D0687575

Leaving Everything Behind

Leaving Everything Behind

The Songs and Memories of
a Cheyenne Woman

by Bertha Little Coyote
and
Virginia Giglio

UNIVERSITY OF OKLAHOMA PRESS
Norman and London

Also by Virginia Giglio
Southern Cheyenne Women's Songs (Norman, 1994)

Library of Congress Cataloging-in-Publication Data

Little Coyote, Bertha, 1912–
    Leaving everything behind : the songs and memories of a Cheyenne
woman / by Bertha Little Coyote and Virginia Giglio.
        p.   cm.
    Includes index.
    Includes compact disc and transcriptions of songs.
    ISBN 0-8061-2984-0 (alk. paper)
    1. Little Coyote, Bertha, 1912– . 2. Women singers—Oklahoma—
Biography. 3. Cheyenne Indians—Oklahoma—Biography. 4. Cheyenne
women—Oklahoma—Biography. I. Giglio, Virginia, 1953– . II. Title.
ML420.L772A3   1997
781.62'973—dc21
    [B]   97–11270
                                                                          CIP
                                                                          MN

Text design by Alicia Hembekides.

The paper in this book meets the guidelines for permanence and durability of the
Committee on Production Guidelines for Book Longevity of the Council on Library
Resources, Inc.∞

1 2 3 4 5 6 7 8 9 10

I leave this in memory of myself
to my family that I love,
my Cheyenne people,
and the Mennonite Church, its pastors and workers
that kept me in line with my belief as a Christian.

Bertha Little Coyote

Dedicated to my beloved teacher, David P. McAllester,
and, with all my heart, to my husband, Neal Dunnigan.

Virginia Giglio

Contents

Illustrations

FIGURES

SONG TRANSCRIPTIONS

PHOTOGRAPHS *(following page 48)*

Bertha Little Coyote, 1930
Girls with legs wrapped for riding
Cantonment School
Girls wearing bullhides, Concho Indian School, 1913
Concho Indian School, 1926
Dust storm, 1930s
Old stone commissary building at Cantonment, 1931
Bertha and her dogs in front of her brush arbor kitchen
Bertha at age thirty-three
Sewing Day at Fonda Church
Bertha Little Coyote with Sioux trick riders
Bertha Little Coyote at Folklife Festival, Washington, D.C.
Bertha Little Coyote, Community Health Representative

Preface

Bertha Little Coyote is a "pistol." That Oklahoma localism incorporates several qualities underscored in Bertha's disposition: she is predictably outspoken, unquestionably courageous, and energetically expressive of opinions that are, to many people's chagrin, piercingly correct in most situations. She is also, as I discovered while working with her on this book, deeply tender-hearted, an expressive and intelligent musician, profoundly insightful, and fiercely committed to people—especially Cheyenne people. She has triumphed over eighty-four years of a difficult life and has full hopes for an exciting spiritual existence after she leaves everything on earth behind.

I introduced myself to Bertha Little Coyote one autumn day in 1989, having driven more than 130 miles west from my home to ask her to help me with my dissertation project, later to become the book *Southern Cheyenne Women's Songs*. As my car pulled up, Bertha walked out to get a good look at me. Her comment: "Oh."

I introduced myself, explaining that I had been told if I wanted to learn about Cheyenne women and their songs, I should come to Bertha Little Coyote. Her reply: "I don't help white women."

Then she invited me to sit, and we talked for two hours.

"Why do they always come to me?" she asked. I didn't understand her question until later, when I discovered that, as this book will show, Bertha has been consulted often and at length about Cheyenne culture and history. She was getting a little tired of it.

For this and for other reasons, Bertha was reluctant to get involved in my original song-collecting project. "I don't help white people" was a statement she reiterated often during our first visit.

Bertha complained that her picture had been used in newspaper articles without her permission. She complained that a photograph of her used in an art exhibition had shown her "looking down like I was ashamed. I've never done anything to be ashamed of in my life." (She told me she walked into the gallery and demanded its removal.)

"And you know what some newspaper reporter said about me?" She looked at me significantly—I knew a test was at hand.

"He said I wasn't afraid to talk to God! Now what do you suppose he meant by that?"

I thought, then smiled and said, "I think he meant that *you* are not afraid of *anyone.*"

"You're right!" she chuckled.

Then we swapped stories about the injustices of the world while we petted the stray kittens who had found a home among the boxes and blankets in Bertha's carport. My own stories centered around loneliness and single parenthood and the tragic death of my mother. Bertha's stories of loss resonated with the suffering that I was just getting old enough to know.

During our first visit I learned a great deal about Bertha Little Coyote. I learned that she was "part white," a Cheyenne description of what others might refer to as half-blood. About the identity of her father, Bertha was not sure. This stigma had affected her childhood among the Cheyenne people, just as being Indian was a cause of derision to her white classmates in public school. She had fought the mean children who had called her "dog-eater"; I would learn that the division of white and red in Bertha's existence is still a perpetual, quiet battle.

She said she would not sing for me. She said she no longer sang well. And she said she really didn't have anything to tell me. So I thanked her for her time, put down a cat, and prepared to leave.

"May I come back?" I asked.

"What for?" she asked in surprise—after all, she had made it plain that she didn't help white people.

"I know that you don't help white people, but I wonder if I could come back and learn from you how I should behave when I visit other Indian people, so that I don't make the same mistakes that other white people have made with you?" She was clearly surprised—and pleased.

"Well, I guess you can come back. But I don't help white people." As I was getting into my car, she walked out and stopped me. "But be sure, when you come back, to knock on my bedroom window. I might be sleeping in there."

Thus began my friendship with Bertha Little Coyote. I never did have to knock on her window. She was always glad to see me, and I to see her.

It really isn't good manners, in Cheyenne custom, to put oneself forward as an expert or to be singled out for special attention. Bertha is not an expert, nor is she, in her own mind, a particularly saintly person. She tries hard. She struggles. When I first I met Bertha, I believed that she held answers for me—answers about how to survive in spite of deep hurts, in spite of the tragic death of loved ones, the betrayal of friends and lovers, in spite of poverty, ill health, and occasional periods of profound spiritual loneliness.

To my surprise and naïve disappointment, I discovered that Bertha was not some sort of unique repository of old Indian wisdom (though her cultural knowledge is wide-ranging and she has lived long and learned much.) Bertha Little Coyote turned out to be just like me. Our relationship became an empathetic confessional, each of us listening to and learning to love the other.

It was the depth of her personality, her power, her particular ability to speak and sing right to the quick of my heart—these were the things convinced me, compelled me, to ask her to let me write a book about her. And she consented in spite of her reluctance to "put herself forward"—a generous and bold move on her part. But as the project grew more and more real, her reluctance gave way to conviction that it was important to tell her story. And that's when this story stopped being biography and became autobiography, and finally a distillation of her life down to the most important memories.

This book contains what Bertha Little Coyote chooses to include. She has chosen not to disclose every life detail. Some of Bertha's stories were for me alone, and I have followed her wishes regarding things that she wants to keep private.

Included, however, are stories about government school, old-time Cheyenne life, fighting white boys, singing around the drum, dancing with the war mothers, being baptized in the lake, and dreaming important dreams. I was most interested in Bertha's singing, for which she has a wonderful reputation among Cheyenne people, and the two of us can be heard singing together on the last compact disc selection.

We were occasionally interrupted during this project, including time out for cataract surgery and a heart attack for Bertha and an out-of-state move and a marriage for me. Visits ranged from one- or two-day runs out from my home in Norman, Oklahoma, to longer live-in visits of a week at a time after I moved to Connecticut in 1993. Bertha's health and stamina became a factor in our ability to gather data for the book, but she gamely endured long interview sessions in her home, on the telephone, and during long drives through western Oklahoma. She has allowed me to sit with her at benefit dances at Fonda Community Hall, dance with her at powwows at Red Moon and Concho, clean off graves with her at Cantonment Cemetery, sing with her at the Seiling Mennonite Church, and bake in the sun with her while looking on at Sun

Dance ceremonies. I taped interviews with her in her home and on long drives in the car while taking her to run errands and to visit friends, and transcribed lengthy telephone conversations.

I also found resources in the work of people who had listened to Bertha before me: a 1989 interview of Bertha taped by Joe Todd of the Oklahoma Historical Society; Daniel Hodges's dissertation research and transcriptions of songs from a recording made by Oscar Humphreys in 1969; and information and hymns from *Tsese-Ma'heone-Nemeotòtse: Cheyenne Spiritual Songs*,[1] for which Bertha served on the editorial committee and as a contributor.

Bertha has taught and touched many people both within and outside the Southern Cheyenne and Arapaho tribes, including those with academic and cultural preservation interests. The intention of this book and its accompanying compact disc is to broaden her audience and to provide an intense visit with Bertha Little Coyote in which she shares her powerful music and memories.

For nurturing this vision with me I am grateful to George Bauer, John Drayton, Kimberly Wiar, and Sarah Iselin of the University of Oklahoma Press. In the light of Bertha Little Coyote's age, the University of Oklahoma Press advanced royalties to Bertha before publication—a rare and humane gesture, much appreciated by Bertha and myself.

I am grateful to William Welge, Oklahoma Historical Society, for permission to incorporate Joe Todd's interview into Bertha's story, to Daniel Hodges for graciously allowing the reprinting of his transcriptions and formal analyses from his 1980 dissertation, to Oscar Humphreys of Indian Records, Inc., for his contribution to the compact disc accompanying this book, and to Bill and Greta Blanton for their Oklahoma hospitality. I thank the Reverends Newton and Amelia Old Crow, pastors, Seiling Mennonite

---

1. David Graber, ed. (Newton, Kans.: Faith and Life Press, 1982).

Church; the Reverend Dr. Wayne Leman, missionary-linguist; the Reverend Father Peter Powell, long-time friend of the Cheyenne people; Sister Mary Margaret Kelly, Illinois State University; and Angela Giglio Andrews for their prayerful support of this project. A special thanks goes to the Reverend Willis Busenitz of the Mennonite Indian Leaders Council, who gave permission for several hymns to be reprinted in this book.

I am indebted to Dr. Donald DeWitt and the staff of the University of Oklahoma Western History Collections; Diane Costin of the El Reno Carnegie Library; copyist Don Wallace, who formatted several song transcriptions using Finale software; Orazio Spagnardi and Nite-Lite Productions for engineering the compact disc master; and George Landis, who restored many of the photographs from Bertha's private collection and the archives of the General Conference Mennonite Church. My family, including my husband, Neal Dunnigan; sons Barnabas and Daniel; and my Cheyenne sister and brother Diane and Burton Hawk, have been of inestimable help during the writing of this book.

A SPECIAL NOTE REGARDING THE COMPACT DISC

The accompanying compact disc is fundamental to understanding the songs and memories of Bertha Little Coyote. (Please see Apendix D, "Compact Disc Notes.") In the book, footnotes will refer you to numbered selections, ordered by their appearance in the text. The songs on the disc are essential to a complete reading of the book, because Bertha's story is a musical as well as an oral narrative.

In appendices A, B, and C, readers who are interested in a visual representation of Bertha's music will find musical transcriptions. The transcriptions represent attempts by several people to capture, within a framework of Western European–based notation, songs from Bertha's repertoire which, when found in their natural state, emanate from an oral/aural tradition. The transcriptions vary in focus and style, and are not guaranteed to match any individual listener's perceptions. They are presented here only as an optional listening guide, and are what Bertha refers to as "white man's note music." With the exception of the hymns, they are not used by her or anyone she knows to learn or teach song melodies or texts.

All notated transcriptions are grouped by source (rather than in compact disc or narrative order). Three sources of transcriptions were used: *Southern Cheyenne Women's Songs*,[2] "Transcription and Formal Analysis of Southern Cheyenne Songs,"[3] and *Tsese-Ma'heone-Nemeotòtse: Cheyenne Spiritual Songs*. Notated transcriptions of Bertha's songs can be helpful to the student of Cheyenne music, but they are an incomplete representation of the sound of her voice or the nuances of her performances. It is therefore essential that one listen to Bertha's music and words.

One warning: some of the recorded selections contain excerpts of conversations between Bertha and me. Regarding these conversations I will admit that my questions were often naïve or badly posed and my learning was slow, but these moments are offered not only for their content but also as a characterization of the relationship between Bertha and me as we strove to understand each other. With these inclusions I hoped to bring you, the listener, into Bertha's home, providing an opportunity to feel what it was like to sit at the feet of this remarkable woman.

VIRGINIA GIGLIO

---

2. Virginia Giglio (Norman: University of Oklahoma Press, 1994).
3. Daniel Houston Hodges (Ph.D. diss., University of Oklahoma, 1980).

Leaving Everything Behind

Chapter One

Catfish Toes and Bullhides

Two centuries before Bertha Little Coyote was born in 1912, Cheyenne families and their horse herds roamed the warm grasslands of the Great Plains, returning at change of season to homesites where they had planted crops for winter use. So expert were they at hunting and preparing the hides of the buffalo, the Cheyennes eventually established a lucrative buffalo robe trade with white pioneer businessmen. The trade thrived until the mid-nineteenth century, when the U.S. government began to define the boundaries within which each Plains tribe could live and hunt. After the beginning of the reservation system, an accelerating sequence of phenomena would change the Cheyenne world forever: trains, gold fever, extermination of the buffalo herds, military engagements, homesteaders, massacres, free range cattlemen, missionaries, and allotment of lands. Disaster followed disaster as a determined political and social power dominated the lives of Cheyenne people, using methods of annihilation, confiscation, and, finally, education.

By the end of the nineteenth century, a succession of government agents, missionaries, and schoolteachers was delegated to reeducate Cheyennes for existence within a society dominated by white cultural values. Policy makers determined that farming and animal husbandry were to be the new economic operations of the Cheyennes, and at boarding schools children were taught white ways of thinking, speaking, cooking, cleaning, dressing, socializing, and worshiping. Schooling—the curriculum as well as the pedagogical methods and their repercussions—had a major impact on the lives of many Cheyenne people still living today.

Bertha Little Coyote entered Cantonment, a government boarding school near Canton, Oklahoma, when she was seven years old (1919). "No more speaking Indian!" she was told. The purpose of the school was to teach white language and behaviors, but another rationale behind the "no Indian" rule is revealed by Bertha as she describes the efforts of teachers to keep order among children of different tribes, all with their own tongues, cliques, and prejudices. Efforts to suppress her native language, however, had an opposite effect on Bertha, whose Cheyenne linguistic identity was tenacious.

In Bertha's recollection of boarding school we find clues to the roles of both boys and girls in the performance of school chores. Strictness of place for women and men was thus communicated; in Bertha's later life we will see that she often abandoned those implanted ideas.

Bertha's school memories contrast the occasional sweetness of the matrons with the rigid army-style discipline by which her life was ordered. Waked from army cots, marched to meals, ordered to chores, schooled by the bell, the children later knelt by their beds to say nighttime prayers out loud and in unison. As one of the few not to succumb to the swine flu epidemic, Bertha found herself with a nurse's duties—a large responsibility for a seven-year-old.

Bertha's memories are not all so grim. She describes acting in plays, making doll clothes and miniature tipis, and joining in girls' games in which she and her classmates explored issues of womanhood as they knew it: nurture, protection, and abandonment. Bertha also describes the play activities of the boys, some of which she "imitated."

We read about weekly hayrides to town to spend government-issued five-dollar checks. The story behind Bertha's curious weekly allowance begins with the 1897 government scheme to acquire Indian lands in

Oklahoma: the Dawes Act. Under this policy, approximately 500,000 Cheyenne and Arapaho acres were parceled into 160-acre units (40-acre units for infants) and distributed to tribe members. A remainder of about 3,500,000 acres were declared a surplus and opened for settlement. For this surplus the government paid the tribes about two and a half dollars per acre. The funds were said to be put in reserve for schools, missions, agencies, and miscellaneous purposes. Apparently, Bertha and her classmates received, on a weekly basis, some of that money, and it eventually found its way into the pockets of town storekeepers.

Bertha found a religion at Cantonment School that would last her life long—Christianity. It might seem curious, in light of today's notions of separation of church and state, that Cantonment School was a government as well as a missionary operation. Assigning missionaries to serve as Indian agents was begun by President Grant and his "Quaker Peace Policy." Grant was convinced that missionaries would be less likely to behave dishonestly among the Indians and were better candidates for responsible positions among them. Each tribe was assigned to a particular denomination.

A generation after the inception of Grant's policy, Bertha's religious training was administered by Mennonite missionaries at Cantonment. Baptized at age thirteen, Bertha believes the disciplined environment of the school and the teachings of the Mennonite missionaries gave her a firm start on the Christian path.

If you go up to Cantonment now, there's no school buildings left. But those cedar trees growing in a row? That shows where they used to live, the employees, in houses there.

When I was seven years old, in 1919, I started school at Cantonment boarding school—government school. All the school children's folks took us September first, and we came home to visit just a few holidays like Thanksgiving and Christmas, New Year's and Easter. There was no Mother's Day in those days. And then maybe they'd let us come home for one day on Memorial Day—Decoration Day, we used to call it. School let out June 30. That was Cantonment when I first started school.

Well, when I first went to school, there were Cheyennes and Arapahos, and we got along pretty good until they started bringing in other tribes. You know, a lot of the Indians kept their children out, they wanted them at home, not at boarding school. Our folks, they pushed us into government school, and we stayed there. And the school was lacking of children, so they asked the other tribes to send children. And they sent Poncas—mostly it was Poncas and Otoes that came that first year. And then if we'd talk Cheyenne or the Arapahos would talk Arapaho (which we did—we didn't lose it—we talked our language even at school—they didn't tell us we couldn't speak it) but it was those other tribes, if they didn't understand, which they didn't, they didn't even know what we'd be talking about, they'd go report us to the matron.

"She was talkin' to so-in-so and I know she was talkin' about me!" And this was too much on the matron and the employees, making a fuss, and it was just trouble, trouble, so they told us, "No more speaking Indian!"

Well, we'd forget and somebody would catch us and report us, and that old matron, she took a washrag and lye soap and she'd say, "You're not supposed to talk Indian!" Mouth washed out! Well, she never got most of them to quit talking Indian.

I wouldn't let them wash my mouth out. I used to run back to the mess hall. I never got that much punishment—I was kind of an obedient child, I was kind of scared that I might get punished for something, or kept away from parties, or have to work off demerits.

I don't think there was more than a hundred of us boys and girls together. There was a big dormitory building at Cantonment—it was just one two-story building we called the school building. The girls lived on the east side and the boys lived on the west side of the building and in between there was a dining hall. The boys ate on one side and the girls ate on the other side of the dining hall, and then the kitchen was on the north end of the dining hall.

We lived on the second floor and all the beds were in a row, and then the matron's room was next to the dormitory. And then across the hall was a hospital, we called it the hospital—anybody get sick they were put in that room.

The other things was in there—the classroom, playroom. On the bottom floor of the school building, the two rooms on the east end were the cook's room and the teacher's room. There was a big area, a big room, they called it a playroom, and they had little tables just so high—just about a foot off the floor. We would play jacks or whatever. Like I said, there wasn't more than a hundred children, so there couldn't be more than fifty girls.

We all dressed alike, for everyday clothes. The boys had shirts, long-sleeved shirts, and knickers. The girls had chambray clothing, what we'd call chambray now, and we'd have what we'd call hickory dresses, which was denim, pin-striped denim, just straight, T-shape. No pockets.

And long stockings. We all wore long, coarse black stockings with catfish toes—we used to call them catfish toes—the seam all coming together like a catfish mouth. And we had black hightop lace shoes, and we called them bullhides cause they was all leather, real good, government issue. They was leather, so we called them "bullhides." There was no such thing as "shoes." We called them bullhides!

At Cantonment, girls were allowed to wear their hair in a braid. Some used soap plant shampoo, yucca root—boil it in water, makes your hair like a raven's back. Indians didn't cut their hair for anything in those old days, only for a good reason. And we all wore ponytails, too, and we had hair clasps—just so we kept it neat, they let us wear it that way.

We had boxes and everybody had a number. All the time I was

at Cantonment, I was Number Two. The matron marked all the clothes. Clothes were supposed to be put in that box—it was just a box like soap, maybe ten by twelve or twelve by twelve. If they found any bit of my clothes laying around that were Number Two, I got punished for it. If somebody left their clothes around, they'd probably have to stay away from a party or have to sweep up the floor, or some "detail" to work off demerits.

As for chores, I was detailed to everything that I could remember. Let's see, my very first job was they had to put me on a stool and I helped wash clothes, that was my first job, and any of the details cleaning the dining area after each meal. If you were assigned to housekeeping you done the cleaning of the house. Everybody had to make their own beds, that bed had to be made up when you got up before you went downstairs into the washroom to clean up for breakfast.

The school had Holstein cows, and that was the boys' job. The boys had different chores from the girls. They would take care of the cows, milk them, and we had a lot of milk. And they'd butcher—that was a source of meat. When I first started they had hogs, but they kept the cows and got rid of the hogs. Maybe the boys did a little farming, but I really didn't pay that much attention to the boys' side of the school.

I was detailed to the kitchen, housekeeping, into laundry where all the sheets and blankets and clothes were washed—they had big washing machines. They'd put all the sheets in that big washer, and then there was a wringer, and the boys would do that. Then there was a mangle, they didn't put them in the dryer, they put them in the mangle, they called it. We would fold them double, and they would put them through that mangle—it was a thing that had padded white sheets on the outside, and a roll, and it would roll the clothes through, and ironed them. Ironed them dry. And then there was a little platform and it would catch it, and we'd fold up the sheet. If you go in my bathroom today and look at my towels, you will see the way I was trained. Fold them this way, fold them that way, and pile them up.

When I was older, I was detailed to help the cook. I'd say I was about ten years old when I started waiting on tables—I had to wait on the employees. I had to help the cook dish out the food, and when she'd dish out I'd carry it to the table, and she taught me how to set the table. She taught me where to put this and that, and then she'd come in and check and see if I had done it right, and then when the employees came in to eat, why it was ready for them. And then I waited on them, if they wanted some more coffee or if they wanted some more bread. Of course there weren't that many employees there. I had a little tray to serve with.

The food was on the table family-style. I served tea, coffee, more bread—I had to watch the table. The employees had vegetables, the school children didn't have all those. The white people was eating on one side and the Indian children was eating over on another side of the room. There was a difference. They gave the Indian children canned potatoes. The government would send big cans, big square cans about two feet high, full of potatoes. I don't know how they preserved them. But the employees they had fresh potatoes. I had to help the cook peel potatoes.

The employees had better bread than the children, homemade bread or biscuits, and they had coffee, tea, fresh eggs, and fresh vegetables and meat. For the children, we mostly had beans and cheese and macaroni. I always say to this day that I don't like macaroni and I don't like cheese. I don't like prunes, dried prunes and peaches, because that was what we had. And the cooks made coarse bread. They had a bread mixer, and it used to mix the bread, and I don't know what kind of yeast they used, but it was kind of coarse bread. The children who were helpers, sometimes we used to eat in the kitchen because we had to run back to school.

We were trained to get up at six. Hear the bell, and everybody get up. I still get up at six today—no alarm clock. The matron would come in. We had a good matron, I'll have to tell you about her. She was heavyset, she had gray hair, and she wore it on top of her head like these heavyset old ladies. And at bedtime she'd say, "All right girls, time to go to bed. Get to your beds, get ready to say your prayers." We'd kneel at the foot of the bed and say, "Now I lay me down to sleep, I pray the Lord my soul to keep, if I should die before I wake, I pray the Lord my soul to take. Amen." And then she'd come down the line and she'd kiss us. All down the line, all of us girls. She was nice. I remember, her name was Mrs. Wolf. And we'd sleep—army blankets, wool blankets, pillows—iron beds.

Up at 6:00, downstairs by 6:15. "Make up your bed, straighten up, make your bottom sheet real nice, and put your blanket on it, and pull your top sheet back like that, a cuff like." Then we'd put our pillow on it. We didn't have bedspreads—the army blanket was on top, and we slept between two sheets. The blanket was army color, tan army color.

At 6:15 we had to go down and wash up. "Hang up your towel!" Numbers on the wall, and your towel is supposed to be hanging there, Number Two, everything was Number Two for me. They didn't have showers, they had tubs—course the tubs had legs on them—I think there was three stalls. Then we had those big bars of lye soap, like the army used to have—I don't think we washed our face with it. I think they gave us Ivory soap to wash our face with.

As for washing up, you know children, they don't take more than a minute to wash up. Just so they get some water on their face, then they're through. It just all depended on how much time you wanted to take, but no more than five minutes. Then we all went back in the playroom and there would be a signal, a bell, we'd all get in there. "Line up!" They went by height. "Company A, Company B, Company C!"

The bigger girls was Company A. In Company A they used to pick out officers, and these officers were assigned to see that everything was running in order. Company A was supposed to be the big sisters to these little ones in Company B—if the little ones needed help, you was supposed to help. It was like a big sister, and that's what they did. And 6:15, somewhere around there, "Get outside, get out there, and start exercising!" Girls on one side, boys on the other, just like I said. Company A was on one side, then Company B and Company C in front of this big building. There was this flower garden, where we tended flowers, then a sidewalk down to the gate going out.

And there was the Boys' Advisor that would stand there—he was Chippewa Indian, he wasn't a superintendent or supervisor, he was a disciplinarian. That was his title. He'd get out there, and he'd say, "Everybody, one, two!" He would count, and we'd start marching. Company A girls took care of Company B girls, and Company B girls took care of Company C girls. And drill. Army! We were in army style! Put me out there today, I could march. I know all them orders, you know, right face! Left face! Right face! Left face!

The bell would ring, and that was for us to go into the dining hall. We'd march in, we knew our place at the table, and we knew where we sat—the same place when we first started school, we were assigned a place. They had a little bell they tapped, you would stand up to the table until everybody was in place, and then they tapped the bell, and everybody sat down. We said our grace, God bless this food. I have forgotten that part, but it was just a little grace that we all repeated. And then they tapped the bell and we started eating.

"How many teeth do you have?" those teachers would say. "You have thirty-two teeth. So you must chew your food one time for every tooth in your head."

There was a bigger girl at one end of the table. There were three girls on each side and one at each end. The plates were already set down. And then they'd pass the food along. I very well remember those dishes—they were oblong— china. That's one thing, we ate out of china and used good silverware. And drank milk—no coffee, no tea. Water and milk.

For breakfast we usually had bread and butter. And then we had oatmeal and we had bacon—it wasn't like we have today, of course, a lot of improvement has been made in food. It was the best at that time. It had to be good grade of food—a better grade, although some of it was coarse and we got tired of it, the same thing over and over. That was the main gripe, that we had too much of one thing too many times—like I said, I don't like macaroni and I don't like cheese and I don't like prunes.

We finished breakfast at twenty minutes after seven. Everybody would clean off their own plate and pass it down. We'd make a pile at the end—there was a dish there for the forks, for the silverware. And then we'd march out, all those who weren't detailed to wash dishes. Some were detailed to stay and help cook. The rest of us marched out to go and get ready for school. Between 7:45 and 8:00 you got ready to go to school.

I think it was about 8:30 or 9:00 we got to the school room, because we were detailed—everybody had to finish their work before school. I'd run—I had to finish my work—and then these others, they would do their work—they'd all finish their work before they went to school. Just like army.

Quarantine! Quarantine! Did you ever hear of quarantine? They used to have quarantines in army barracks, and we used to have them, too. Someone get measles, everybody was quarantined, that's the way it was at Cantonment. They would fence around the building and have a night watchman. Nobody came through there unless the watchman knew who was coming through. They watched us children.

And our folks would come in wagons—there were roads and there was a bridge going down to the river. And if there was a quarantine, our folks, even if they come to the gate, they'd be turned away. We were quarantined.

We had an old government doctor—I don't remember him much. But like I said, across the hall from the matron's room was the sick room, and in those days, if maybe one or two had pneumonia, or whatever, they were placed in that room until they were able to get up. Of course children, they don't like to lay in bed, you know, they want to get up and play whether they feel like it or not, so they didn't stay in bed very long. But them that were very sick, they put them in that hospital—boys and girls both. I helped to take care of them. I was kind of like a little nurse, anyway.

And then 1919, that's when the flu epidemic hit Cantonment. I must have been seven years old—I had to be seven years old to be able to wait on them. Everybody was sick, all the people was sick, I was the only one who didn't get sick. The employees were sick, everybody was sick excepting for an old Indian man and this other old white man—the dairy man—his name was Hank Ashpaugh.

We made soup for the sick people. They had big aluminum kettles, and they'd put the chunks of meat and let it boil. We had a big range—it was one big range, and they'd put all those kettles on that and they'd put those chunks of meat and let it boil. Then when it was done, why, they'd get these forks and knives and get the meat out. We didn't feed these sick people meat. We fed them hard tack—there was no soft crackers like now, we had hard tack, we called it hard tack—and we served them hard tack and a bowl of soup, broth. We gave it to whoever wanted to eat, but most of them was too sick, they couldn't eat.

And the men would carry it up these flights of stairs, and then I'd help take soup and crackers to the sick ones, and take them their spoons, the ones that wanted to eat. And some died. Of course I didn't see them die, but we lost four, I'd say no more than five out of the whole school. But there was some pretty sick girls up there, and my friend was one of them that died—maybe they would have gotten cured if they'd stayed. But some of them, they had an Indian doctor, and some of the parents came up and got their children and took them home to be Indian doctored. And I think my friend, she was one of them that got taken home—she passed away.

Anyway, it was like that, me and those men working alone, for about a day, day and a half, and then some of the employees and some of those kids felt better so they could get back up and do some of the work. So, that was the flu epidemic.

When I went to Cantonment school, I had to start from primer, first grade. That took one year. And some of them, it took them two years to learn the alphabet, and some it just took one year to finish primer and first. We had big letters: A, B, C, and you had to learn to read and to recognize them. And we took penmanship. We were graded by that, penmanship. And that penmanship, they made you sit there. And I think we were all good writers, you could read our writing. Nowadays, most people all write like doctors.

We'd have classes from 9:00 to 11:30. We used to get out at 11:30 or quarter to twelve, long enough to get back to the building—the school building was separate from the big building. We'd go back over there, "Wash your hands!" Bell ring, twelve o'clock, "Go eat your lunch!"

It was twenty-five minutes to eat, or maybe we had a little more time to eat at noon, then leave the table, same thing, go through the same thing. Say our prayer and everything. And then we had a little time to play until one o'clock. As soon as you get your dinner over with, then you could play. And then one o'clock we'd get back to school again.

Our classes? They always found something for us to do. We had arithmetic, we had English, we had penmanship, we had history. We had to learn all the multiplication tables when I was in third grade, and I still remember it. Oh, and they kept us till we learned it. If you couldn't get that multiplication table, if you didn't learn your "nines," you were assigned to learn that at night until you learned it. You learned it! They *made* you learn it!

So we'd stay there until four o'clock and then I think that supper was at 5:00 or 5:30. I don't remember just exactly what time, anyway, I think it was 5:30, "Line up again for supper!"

After supper, sometimes we'd have picture shows. And on Saturday night we had a party. Friday night was the movie, and they had a pump piano and this roller would make music for silent pictures. The piano was on the side, and some of the bigger girls would get up there and pump that piano with that roller—you've seen those—and that's the kind of music we had.

And we'd sit there and watch that movie, and that was the music. Of course we had a lot of plays and activities like that—they always managed to have something like that—we'd all learn our parts. I guess that they done a lot of that because you know Indian is kinda shy—won't speak out—but they had a lot of programs like that where you had to be on stage, and you'd get up there and perform.

Oh, they'd just put me in everything on the stage. I remember very vividly. There was this doctor's son, they were white you know, and he played a doctor, and I was the mother, I had a baby, and then this girl was a nurse. And the doctor he comes to see my baby and I was sitting there in a rocking chair with my baby and he says, "What seems to be wrong with your baby?"

I just hollered, "Oh, something must be wrong with my baby! Oh, it just cries and cries all the time!" I had to look at my baby and I could hear them giggling. Them boys would giggle at us girls when we'd try to do something in a play. And I said my baby was so sick or something. And he said, "I believe your baby's got pneumonia." And I cried, "You mean my baby's gonna die?" You could hear that laughter! I just remember that one part. I don't remember all of it, any other plays I was in, but I used to be in lot of plays.

And when we played outside, we never did get away from our Indian life. We used to play with little dolls made of rags, doll rags, we called them. We'd get a piece of white material and make a ball about the size of marble, not too big, like nickel size. From that we'd make a head and cover it with a piece of black material all raveled down, like black hair was black. Then we'd cut out T-shape dresses, you didn't sew them, you'd fold it over and make a hole for the head, then tie it around a rag body. We'd secure the rags under the dress.

Then we'd make babies for our dolls, with black cloth over their head like the mother. Then we'd take a strip maybe three to four inches long and inch wide, and on one side we'd hem and gather it up like a little sleeve to make a dress for the baby. The baby would have its head sticking out of the gathered part, and it could stand up alone.

And we'd make little cradles, Cheyenne style. We'd wrap the babies up on a piece of cardboard with rags. We never made man dolls. Later on maybe they did, but during my day, when I used to play doll rags, we didn't make a man doll. If someone said, "This is the husband to your doll," it would just be sticks. We must have already known that the babies didn't have fathers—just like today!

I guess we didn't know how babies got here. And we had little boxes to put all our doll rags in. And we'd get nice printed material, open it and we'd make it big enough to fit our rag doll, plus extra for fringe. We'd unravel that cloth all around for fringe, maybe a half inch or longer, and put it on the doll—that was our doll shawl.

Those doll rags were all we had for our dolls. Beads were scarce—mothers wouldn't let us play with beads. But we made wagons for our dolls out of matchboxes. We'd play family style, we'd visit back and forth, and we'd even make our little tipis out there and we'd just sit out there and enjoy that—just visit one another. That'd be pretty near all afternoon, we'd play rags.

And then we'd have drop the handkerchief, tag, all the children's games that children play, and there was an Indian game we used to play: "The Mother and the Coyote."

We'd choose one to be our mother and the rest of us would hold on to each other around the waist, making a long string. The first one would hold the mother around the waist and the mother would spread her hands, waving them left and right to protect her babies. Before beginning the game the children picked up weeds to resemble food for the coyote, and then the coyote would run right and left and try to touch the babies. If he touches you, you are out of the game. And the mother, she would holler and hold some of his food, throw it at him, try to keep him away by leading the line of children right and left and all around. So the children would keep passing the mother the food, and after she run out, that was the game, coyote got all of us.

"Coyote, here's your food!" she'd holler. But he wanted that child, and we'd swing back and forth, she'd go right and left and left and right to keep the coyote from catching them. Coyote had to get each of the children, starting with the last one, because it was the tail. The mother couldn't protect all of us. And it was fun, and we'd try to dodge that coyote, because when he'd touch you, even just tapping, you were out of the game. When the food was all out, coyote got all of us.

The coyote was just anybody that wanted to be, same with mother. Somebody would holler, "I want to be the coyote!" and that's how it worked.

I really didn't think about my name being Coyote, like in the game. There were a lot of coyote names in them days—Walking Coyote, Coyote Man, a lot of those old Indian names are gone. The people that carried those names are all gone.

And we'd play jacks—we was good in jacks—lot of girls would play jacks, and get twenty, twenty-five jacks at one time. I could get a whole bunch in my hand. Get a whole bunch at one time, "back hand" we called it. Of course we had jump rope, and we'd imitate the boys, play marbles. Those boys, they'd play baseball—make their own baseball out of rags balled up and around and around. And the school had swings, and they had bars, monkey bars I guess they called them, and a teeter-totter.

On Saturday, we'd get our checks and go into town. That old stone building that used to be old Fort Cantonment, Indian Territory, that's still there—that's where we got our checks. That's where the soldiers were, and when the soldiers left it, they converted it to an Indian agency. It was the office where they made leases, and that's where they made their checks out to them if they had any money on account of the government issuing money to the Indians to pay for land around Cantonment. Cheyennes and Arapahos, we got paid $365.00 apiece, $5.00 per week, and we'd take it into town, and spend it. We used to get a $5.00 check—everybody got a $5.00 check every Saturday.

We'd go to town on a hayride. The dairy man, Hank Ashpaugh, had two horses, bay spotted, and he prized those horses something. That was his love! And he hooked them up to a hayrack, and we'd gather, no chairs, no way to sit down—you stood up and held on to the hayrack. Oh, I remember those horses! They were pretty, pretty spotted big horses. One was Spot and one was Ribbon. He hitched them up and we'd all pile in, all the girls. The boys, they'd go in another load.

It was about five miles to Canton, and we'd all have our checks to spend in the town on a Saturday. We'd say, "Hank, sing! Let's sing!" All that old man would sing was "In the Sweet By and By." And we'd sing "In the Sweet By and By" all the way to town. His old chewing tobacco kind of run down his face, you know, and we never thought anything about it—that old man he was good to us, and he took care of us.[1]

When we got to town, let me tell you I bought candy! My brother would meet me and my check and he'd say, "Let's go in here and cash it." Maybe I'd buy gingersnaps—they used to be in a barrel—I don't remember how big that barrel was, but it was like a pickle barrel, and that thing used to be full of gingersnaps. That's what we'd like to take back to school—of course everything was

---

1. Compact disc selection 1: Story and Song, "In the Sweet By and By" [4:09]

cheap back then. Crackerjack, candy! You could get a whole bag of candy! And whatever change was left, I guess my brother'd take it—and candy, that's all I'd get. Then, "In the Sweet By and By" all the way back to Cantonment.

You know, I remember singing "In the Sweet By and By," but I don't remember any Indian song from my childhood days at Cantonment. Of course, we didn't practice them when I went to school, and there wasn't many children songs when I was little. And at that time, I wasn't interested in learning round dance songs or other kinds.

Sunday morning, church. Sunday night, church. And Thursday night was church night. On church night, we marched to church. Everywhere we went we marched. "*One!* Two! Three Four! *One!* Two! Three Four! Keep in step! *March!* Two! Three Four!" Everybody kept in step in them bullhides and black stockings. I can just see those little feet go up. And then "Sit down!" Then there was a prayer, and everybody had a song book, we'd all sing.

The preacher, his wife played the piano. The preacher would preach, say prayers. At Christmas, sometimes we took part in plays like they have today: the manger, shepherds, angels. They still have the same way of doing it now that they did those days. And on Easter we'd hunt eggs. The employees would color eggs and hide them and we'd all go and hunt eggs. Then of course on Decoration Day, what they call Memorial Day now, they'd take us out walking and we'd pick wildflowers and we'd put them on the graves.

There was a cemetery close by which is still there. Some of those graves were people we knew and some we didn't—we just put flowers for everyone. Lot of Indians had their own private cemeteries—family cemeteries. Nowadays, most of them are lost. But that Cantonment Cemetery was for everybody. It was first established by the Mennonites. The Mennonites were the first ones to establish a school there for the Indian children, especially the Cheyenne children in the Cheyenne territory. Now the rest of those Cheyennes went to Darlington Government School down by El Reno. But Cantonment was a mission school. The workers of the Mennonites built a church there, there wasn't many of them at the time. Then a lot of those old missionaries died and they're buried there with the Indians.

The Mennonites let other denominations preach there at the church. Sometimes there was a Baptist preacher. Most of the time when I was at Cantonment, the preacher was a Mennonite, because he was the only preacher around.

In those Cantonment days, that was when I was baptized into the Mennonite Church—on May 30, in 1925, the last year I went to school there at Cantonment. I was a sixth grader. Some Ponca girls were baptized along with me. I think there were ten of us, and I think even the preacher's son was baptized the same time I was baptized. And that's how long I've been a Mennonite, and I don't intend to change.

At Cantonment, most of the teachers were white, just a few were Indian. The teachers, they had to have more schooling than the regular employees, like the laundry workers, the cook, and the matron. As for how the teachers liked the students, some they liked and some they didn't like. Nowadays, you know, there's supposed to be no discrimination.

Of course, I was a child. I didn't know hate. I didn't know how to hate, and if maybe the teacher wasn't especially kind to me, as a child maybe I overlooked it. But at some point we all got blamed for something, we all did something wrong, we all got punished.

As I look back on Cantonment, I think some of the employees were abusive. Not hitting us or anything, but just the way they treated us—some got punished for nothing. Some of them were not treated equal, not all just alike. The teachers had their pets. Even in public school. That's the way it was, that's the way it still is.

But I think that even though Cantonment was strict and abusive, I was taught to take orders, to mind, to be obedient. And I think that's where my Christian life started. That preacher and his wife, they were stern. They'd come to town and if they saw you coming from the theaters they'd go "Tsk, tsk, tsk!" In those days the Mennonites didn't like movies—I don't know about now.

I was at Cantonment up until sixth grade because that was as far as it went, that was in 1925. Then I went to Longdale public school for seventh grade, but I didn't pass. I was too busy fighting the white kids.

Chapter Two

Feisty Second Soprano

Bertha's school days continue with tales of verbal harassment by male schoolmates in public school. We see a contrast between the feisty Bertha and more timid companions on whose behalf she was always ready to fight—with words or fists.

Bertha's description of her formal music education after returning to government school at Concho, Oklahoma, reveals interesting things about the methods and repertoire of music teaching in Indian boarding school. She found confidence in her singing ability in this setting and also learned to waltz and foxtrot, handling herself diplomatically in party situations. Bertha also learned to give herself homemade tattoos, a fad among Concho schoolgirls.

Bertha expresses regret that her school opportunities extended only as far as graduation in the ninth grade and that sickness prevented her from attending Haskell Indian School. At that point her mother stepped in, arranging for a peyote prayer meeting to be held on her behalf. This is the first mention of Cheyenne ceremony applied to Bertha's life, but for Bertha it is not incongruous with Christian belief or practice.

Another Cheyenne tradition with which Bertha became familiar was hand game, a form of recreation accompanied by a song repertoire all its own. Two bone beads, one marked and the other unmarked, are hidden in a player's hands; a guesser competes by attempting to find the marked bead. Hand gaming is played by two teams who alternate hiding and guessing; small drums accompany the hand game songs. Bertha points out the typical roles of men and women in this setting and how she has, on occasion, stepped into a man's role in the hand game.[1]

Those white boys used to call us gut eaters, you know. "Gut eaters!" "Dog eaters!" "Yellow!" "Squaw!" And that would make me mad. I'd go up to them—I was feisty—any white kid, boy or girl, I would go up to them.

"Gut eaters! Do you eat bologna?" I'd say, "That's guts!" I was feisty. I took up for myself as an Indian, and I would fight.

At the Longdale Public School there were these two mean white boys. One used to comb his hair just slick. He was red-headed and had a freckle face, and I'd fight him. And on the bus there was a boy so bad—he used to pick on one Indian girl all the time. She wouldn't talk. She didn't have much to say, and he'd go pick on her.

"You still eat guts? Do you eat dog?" And she wouldn't talk, it would embarrass her. She'd sit in a corner, and I imagine that affected her in the schoolroom—she never got much schooling. The teachers couldn't get anything out of her, she wouldn't talk. She had to quit school because the children teased her.

So I'd wait until that teasing boy got off of the bus and I'd grab him. And of course, the boy, he'd get away sometimes. But if I got hold of him real good, I used to beat him up. Later I found out he became a bootlegger, and I found out that the other boy I used to fight died, and you know I kind of wanted to go to his funeral, but I didn't get to go.

There was one boy, our government doctor's boy—he was kind

1. For more information about the history, materials, and song repertoire of hand game, see chapter 3 of *Southern Cheyenne Women's Songs.*

of a girl-acting boy. He used to come across a bridge with me to come to school, calling me names, and one day I pretty near threw him over that bridge. I beat those mean white boys up. I took up for the Indians.

I still do. All of my years I have taken up for my Indian blood. I just fight! They better not call me a name. I'll show them my fists. One time when I was with some Cheyenne people in a cafe, this white lady at another table just stared at us. When we got up to leave I said, "What do you think we are? Monkeys?"

Nowadays, it's not white children who are mean about Indians—it's the parents that discriminate against the Indians. The younger Indians today, they have a fine school, no discrimination, and they come here with white children and visit me in my home. The children get along. But in my school days, the parents taught them to say mean things about Indians. There's still a few white people that discriminate—Communists! I call them Communists!

You know, they say that Al Capone was here in Longdale, Oklahoma—he was a big gangster. It was a rough town, and I heard some people say they drank with Al Capone. It's still a small town, a rough-looking town.

As we grew older and those boys had grown up, they recognized me. We were friends when we met then, when we were older, and so we forgot about the boxing that we used to do back when we were kids. But back then, when they used to call us, "You dirty Indians!" Boy, when they'd start talking like that, I was mean. I'd choke 'em standing up. But the more I fought, the more they thought it was fun, so I quit, and they quit.

So after the seventh grade I left Longdale School and went to Concho School—a government school. Fall of 1927 I went to Concho School for two grades, eighth and ninth. That's as far as I went, ninth grade. If I could have, I would have gone on.

I was in a quartet to sing on the program at graduation. I used to be in a lot of programs to sing—I had a good voice—second soprano.

We had a music teacher, and I think she taught me how to use my singing voice. She just made me sing. I'm natural at singing, but she would go like this, move her hand, start all of us. And she could tell when you were out of tune. "You get in tune, you're the wrong note!"

She never told me that. Well, I knew the song, I could sing it. English songs, second soprano. Too long ago to remember any tunes. At Concho School they picked out some boys and girls to be in choir. That's when our teacher classed us where we belong, that's when I was second soprano.

I'd say there wasn't that many students in the choir. I'd say maybe twelve, fifteen—mixed boys and girls. More girls than boys, that's because boys didn't want to get up on the stage and sing.

We were organized like any other choir. The music teacher can tell what kind of voice you had and put you there. There was first soprano, second soprano, alto, and I think that was the three voices of ladies—girls. And then the bass, tenor—boys.

Our music was nice. Not all religious, but we never had all this commotion that these young people have—dirty, sexy—wasn't like that. Songs about nature, things like that. Every song belonged to its own category.

And we sang programs. The employees, and students, they'd come. We had a chapel, we had an auditorium that was our chapel, too, when I was at Concho. And they played basketball, and they'd put on programs there, and we'd have Sunday school there, and church there. There was no separate church building. All the activities were in that one building, all taking turns using it.

Just think, when I was going to school, we memorized "Village Blacksmith" and Abraham Lincoln's "Gettysburg Address." I could memorize those big addresses like that, and now I can't even remember names.

For our programs we had special Sunday dresses to wear, and shoes. But any other time we all dressed alike, and our shoes were all alike. But like going to a social dance, when we would have our parties, then we could dance with our boyfriends, and then we could put on our own clothes, shoes, everything.

I wouldn't refuse a boy who came and asked me to dance. There were all these old-time dances that white people do, we knew them. But nobody liked to do them. We did waltz, but nobody didn't care to do foxtrot. They call it foxtrot. Like a flea jumping around!

We were taught manners. And we had employees watching, and the boys had their disciplinarian watching. We were watched all the time.

A boy would say, "Would you dance with me?" or, "Can I have the next dance?" or, "Can I have this dance?" whatever. If I didn't want to dance with him, well, maybe I'd have an excuse. I wouldn't want to tell him, "I'd rather not." I'd say, "Go ask somebody else, there's Ellie sitting over there, go ask her to dance with you," or something like that.

We were all in a group you know, and we could sit with our boyfriends, like I said, and we had our chaperons. You stayed there nearly and hour and a half or so. No violence, no going out of the building. No smoking. If the boys smoked they had to go away, down by Caddo Springs, beyond that. I don't know what they would do to you if you were caught. It wasn't allowed, smoking.

Usually Friday night was party night. There were no records. They had a player piano. You know, they'd pump. And they'd have those rolls, that's the way it was. The boys would pump, or the teachers—we always had somebody watching—we never were left alone, we had disciplinarians, matrons, teachers.

We didn't sing out loud during our parties at Concho, you know, we'd just listen to that music. I must have been about ninth grade, I was every bit sixteen years old, maybe seventeen.

Then we had graduation. In my graduation class there were five girls and four boys—we were the first graduating class out of Concho. All the girls just wore what they could afford to wear.

They didn't dress alike, they just wore what they could get—of course they looked nice. I forgot what kind of dress I had on when I graduated.

And that was all at Concho, they didn't have anything more. When I was done, the superintendent said, "Well, Bertha, you've got your baloney now."

I wanted to go on to Haskell School. But the doctor told my mother, "You let her go off to school, she'll come back home to you in a box." That's because they found out that I had tuberculosis, and I had to go to the hospital. And while I was in the hospital, I got this appendix attack came upon me.

My mother she loved me so much. I think I was special to her. I was already at the hospital, and they found that I was to have an appendix operation. And so, when I let my mother know they were going to operate on me, she vowed that she was going to put up a prayer meeting—a peyote meeting. My mother made that vow when I was operated on way back in 1933—an operation was something serious.

They called the peyote meeting a "prayer meeting night." And they did it in my behalf, and she would have members of the group come in and pray for me, that this operation would be a success that I would come out of it. In those days, in 1933, an operation to open you up, you didn't know whether you were going to make it or not. And that's the only time I went to a peyote meeting, but I sat in that meeting all night. You have to sit in there all night, and that was the only time I ever went to a peyote meeting, but they have good music.

So I just had a ninth grade education. What's got me anywhere, is that I'll talk to anybody. Sometimes I get pretty ornery, but I tell it like it is.

Sometimes folks ask about these tattoos on my left hand. That's all foolishness. I made those at Concho School when I was about fourteen or fifteen. Girls made these homemade tattoos. First you mark something with a pencil, then you take a sewing needle, and we'd just pick on that skin that we drew over, and keep punching. We'd punch that pencil lead in there. It hurt, but after a while it gets numb.

That tattoo business was just foolishness. We had nothing else to do so we tattooed ourselves. Most of the girls at school did it. Those homemade tattoos, they fade out if they didn't put enough pencil mark.

But my other tattoos were done by those people that travel with a carnival. They had their own little tent, beside the side show, and they used to tattoo. This lady she had a little tent there, and that's where I went and had tattoos. There was about three of us girls who went in there and had tattoos. It didn't even cost but fifty cents. Back then, I guess Indian girls liked tattoos.

It doesn't embarrass me to tell about my tattoos, but it makes me feel queer—it makes me feel foolish. I shouldn't have done it. There was lots of tattoos done back then. I never give it a second thought that it was on there for life. I thought maybe it could wear off, but it sure didn't. It makes me feel guilty, but, no, there ain't nothing I can do about it, it's there to stay.

Back then, when I was getting to be a young woman, I learned to play hand game. It's kind of a social, and I sang. I never played this at Cantonment School or at Concho—I played it when I was a young woman. Certain people had the sticks, not everybody had them. There was some kind of ritual you went through—fasting— to gain the ability to handle these sticks, or to say you owned those sticks. And you had to ask that person to conduct the hand game.

A long time ago, the Cheyennes were given these guessing sticks. There was a pointer with feathers about four inches long which we would swing back and forth as a pointer, and there were game sticks, I think there were eight. A player that missed had to give up a stick and then on down the line, and bring the buttons across to her side. The buttons went back and forth.

There was no limit—sometimes four games, sometimes eight.

Never less than four—we had too much fun. For after, we'd all bring something to eat, pudding, rice. Just a kind of lunch—frybread, biscuits, soup, meat, rice, wild plum pudding, chokecherry pudding—that was our lunch after the hand game. It was a good get-together.

Like I said, it's a kind of game that we played like a social. They had the drummers, and the hand game songs that would go with the hand game. "Zi do ii via" was one of the songs. That was our enjoyment. You make motions with your hands, back and forth, or however, and sing, "This button that I have in my hand is flying around, flying around," and you're supposed to guess which hand I have it in. And it was a lot of fun—I've played off and on all my life. I played recently, right before Christmas 1995.[2]

We used to play "trash hand game." We'd bet beads or a piece of buckskin. We'd use anything for a bet. There was more of a challenge when we saw something we wanted to win, and we'd pick out who we'd play and they put their bet down. The opponents put something down, one on one. Drummers and songs—two drummers, one on our side and one on their side. When we played, our drummer would sing. And when we lose, the hiding beads and drum would go to the other side.

For hand game, they use little round drums, not those great big drums you always see at dances. Hand game drums just have one side covered with hide, with a string used to hold on that rawhide. And they'd stretch that string across the other side of the drum, and that would be the handle. They'd hit the drum with drumsticks.

Women never play the drum unless we have fun by ourselves. I remember one time there were no man drummers—well, there was one man but he wouldn't sing. So I said, "Let's get it!" So I played that drum. Maybe it was one song over and over but we had fun.

---

2. Compact disc selection 2: Hand Game Song, "Flying Around" [1:43]; see also transcription 1, appendix A.

This song, "O go gi, Mo i ha ni," I sang it slower for the recording to make the words and melody clear. It means, "Crows and magpies will fly in when I'm hand gaming."[3]

The whole team sings along. When two hid beads and one got guessed, she didn't play anymore, but the other was allowed to go on. Then if she's found out, then her team loses the bones. Both teams can sing if they want—wave their hands, distract the guesser. Just play like you felt. If you felt happy, it's enjoyable, and I know I was waving my hands for nothing. And we'd try to distract the guesser.

Hand game is a one-night deal, but bingo, no, that's gambling. I like to use my money for something else. And cards? Cards call you. You play four or five games, you waste time.

Now this modern hand game, like the Kiowas play, they bet, you know, and they bet against each other. Here locally, we challenged the Arapahos, we said, "Come on up!" And they came with their sticks and we played hand game, and the guesser on our side would go down the line and collect, and we bet a dollar apiece and she kept track of it, and if we won, she'd give the money out. Our side would say, "We got twenty dollars!" before they started—that's the modern way. You bet. Boy, did we have fun. There were just about four or five on our side, but pretty soon the backward kind—the kind that sits in the back at dances and doesn't participate—even they were getting their chairs to join in. I won about seven dollars off them Arapahos.

3. Compact disc selection 3: Hand Game Song, "Crows and Magpies" [1:36]; see also transcription 2, appendix A.

Chapter Three

Sweetheart, Lullaby Singer, and War Mother

The settings of Bertha's memories of young womanhood, motherhood, and World War II activities are Fonda and Seiling in western Oklahoma. She details the courtship roles of men and women and the complex arrangements for a Cheyenne wedding. In recognizing a marriage, elaborate ceremonies of giving and receiving presents are customary; Bertha's lifetime of memories is suffused with the Cheyenne tradition of "giving away."

Bertha makes clear to us that there are some experiences, including her first marriage, that she has reserved for her own private recollection—we are not welcome there. But she sings the song and shares the memory of her son's infanthood; she describes the proper care of the dried umbilicus—different for boys than for girls—as well as a way to construct a cradle from materials at hand. Her memories of raising her baby include fighting the dust that permeated Oklahoma homes during those Dust Bowl days. Although those times were difficult, hospitality to those in need was the rule, another kind of giving away.

Bertha's cultural notions regarding women's breasts are, in her opinion, an example of the difference between Cheyennes and whites. She comments upon proper (and improper) dress for young women and differences between Cheyenne and white displays of affection. Her loving relationship with her second husband, Horace, is described, not omit-

ting his struggle with alcohol but including fond memories of living in a tent as newlyweds, taking turns singing songs to amuse each other, and joyfully adopting his grandbaby Clifford as their own son.

After Horace was drafted during World War II and Bertha wanted to visit him at camp, they were forced to legalize their marriage, since Indian weddings, no matter how elaborate or well witnessed, were not then recognized by the government. During World War II, Bertha was chairman of the Fonda Seiling War Mothers, a service club formed to support all those in the Allied forces through prayer and honor dances. Bertha describes the club's activities and their dancing shawls; she shares with us details about the song composed for the group in hopes that people will learn it and keep it going—but properly. She remarks upon the revival of service clubs in Cheyenne communities, describing the differing roles of men and women in carrying out club activities. Bertha also shares with us a dream that she received during wartime in which she played a crucial role in the protection of American soldiers.

An interesting digression in her story reveals details of Cheyenne horsewomanship, and finally Bertha shares some of her last memories of Horace, including his death and funeral, and states her conviction that she will see him again. Bertha goes on to describe the wedding gift she gave to my husband and me, providing insight into another aspect of giving away: a valuable gift can be old and used, its worth based on memories, good wishes, and affection.

Cheyennes say if a girl whistles, she wants a man. There's an old sweetheart song—it's a girl trying to get her sweetheart to be jealous of her. She's telling him she was going to get married, and he says, "I don't care, go ahead and have four husbands if you want."[1]

Those old Wolf Songs, they were dedicated to your sweetheart. I

---

1. Compact disc selection 4: Sweetheart Song [1:55]; see also transcription 3, appendix A.

don't know why it's called a Wolf Song, I guess it's because a man's a wolf! It's Indian way to put animal characteristic in song. Of course, lots of Indian words might not be meant in the way of English translation, but we used to call them "woof" songs. But what is the definition of w-o-o-f—what is the definition? There's no definition—dogs bark, or "woof!" What is that, I don't know—they just called that a woof song, and I just figured it was an animal song, "wolf song." They called those songs *hut ni,* that's the animal "wolf" in Cheyenne.

Now that sweetheart song about "go ahead and have four husbands if you want," I would say that sounds like a jealous song. Oh, they had all kinds of songs like that. I guess, in the evening, up away from the camp you could hear them boys singing them kinds of songs, and the girls would recognize the boy that was singing, recognize their song. Girls sang, too, but we didn't sing them like those boys sing them. I didn't sing them to no boy. Mostly, they're just love songs. They didn't put no names in those songs, they're just love songs.

A boy took a girl home to their camp to indicate that she was to live with him as a wife. He took her to his mother's camp, and the mother used to welcome her new daughter-in-law—really be glad that someone would have their son, I guess. Yes, they used to be glad, really be glad that their son brought a girl home.

Now, this Indian wedding day, they prepare for it. All the relatives, especially a boy's sisters, brothers, and cousins, aunts—all his relatives—they start preparing for the wedding day, Indian wedding day. They set a day—get with the girl's folks and set a day when they would have this wedding and so, when they agree on one certain day, then they would meet at one certain place.

Now the camp of the boy's folks, oh, it used to be so many yards away from that girl's folks' camp—not too far. Then they'd prepare the girl, they'd even give horses away, the boy's folks would give horses. These were presents to that girl's family—and shawls, food—I mean, staples, I guess: coffee, flour, everything. Shawls, dress material, each one, they were labeled, "This was given by so-in-so"—it would be on the shawl, and whatever she wanted to give with that shawl and material: flour, sugar, coffee, shortening, whatever. For every one of those relatives, there was a present. And they'd have the mother, she'd have her share—she'd have more to give to the new in-laws. And horses, maybe his brother give a horse, his uncle, anyway, they used to have horses—ponies—riding ponies.

And so, when the wedding day came, they'd have all these things ready, and they'd start out. And an elderly lady would lead the horse that they put the girl, the bride, to ride on. So this lady would lead the horse with the girl riding, and these others that was giving the presents would follow, and there used to be a wagon would follow with the gifts. They'd all go to the site of the girl's mother's camp, and there they'd have a big canvas spread out there to put these presents and food on. And then the menfolks would take care of the horses—ponies—they'd tie them over there. Then they'd start distributing presents.

The girl's mother, she had to put up a tipi, and bedding for the couple—towels, water bucket. So every present from the girl's side, well, there would be a present from the boy's side to meet it. They used to make a list—if you bring a tent, or a tipi, you was the first one they'd call. The girl's folks would be first, and the one on the girl's family's side—supposed to be her mother—that brought the tipi or tent, why someone from the boy's side would have a present—shawl or whatever—to meet that present. First the tent, then moccasins and quilt to go with the tent. And that was their part to pay for what they got—the shawl and the dishes and food—that was meeting presents. So when they'd call the name to get their present, they'd come out and get it.

The calling order was first the ones that brought the tipis and tents, and then those that brought money. (If you brought a tent as a present, they used to set the tents up.) Those that brought tents (or money), when their names were called, they would come up to meet the present that they was going to take back. So that's the way it was, each one gave something, and each one got some kind of present, or food, like groceries, and of course dry meat was plentiful.

Dry meat is deer meat, sliced, hung out in sun to dry. The way we cook it, we roast it, and then we pound it, and then we heat it with shortening, and also we boil it with salt, it's good. You'd get real constipated if you ate it without a little shortening. It takes a long time to get soft, some soak it overnight. But nowadays I've got pressure cooker, and I wash it good and put it in the pressure cooker. And it's real good. At the wedding, everybody got dry meat.

Now, for Indian wedding, the boy furnishes ponies, wedding gown, and gifts to meet presents brought by the girl's family (like shawls, dress material, food.) And the menfolks take care of the horses, and the gifts to meet the horses. On the boy's side, whoever wanted to pick a horse, a pony, they'd already tell what they was going to meet it with—another horse, or money, or even a gun would be considered to be a gift of a horse. And that was their business over there—the menfolks—they'd tend to that—they'd call the people up and the ponies was given away.

Then when the gifts were all distributed and taken, and then the boy's side, they'd wait. And these on the girl's side would make a meal—cook up something. And they'd take it over there to the boy's folks, along with moccasins, and quilts. And then they'd eat—that was the wedding food. And to whoever brought the groceries for the meal, why they would get the moccasins or quilt. Everything, every present, was met, one way or the other. No drum, no singing at Indian wedding—the folks just exchange gifts all day like it was recognizing who the family was and everything.

I wore a buckskin dress, yeah, a buckskin dress and beaded leggings and moccasins. I don't think I rode a horse, I think somebody led it for me. It was proper to just to walk on the side of whoever is leading the horse—it's proper to walk and not ride.

My first mother-in-law, it wasn't really his mother, it was his aunt—but she was really glad to see me. But my first husband, I told him, "You like to run away." I don't want to talk about my first marriage—I don't even want to talk about it. Six years—1930 to 1936. I don't want to include it in this book. Later, I married Horace Little Coyote and took his name. I should have kept my mother's name, though, Stanton. My mother, she kept her maiden name, which was Eva Stanton, and never took the name of Black Beard after her husband.

My son Woodrow was born in August 1931. Back then, we didn't use bottles, we nursed our babies. We rocked them from side to side, and we'd sing, just keep repeating like that. And I guess it was music to the baby, no words in it. It was just the melody, they liked that, and they'd go to sleep. They used to sing these little Indian lullabies. There's other baby songs, too, but this one has no words in it.[2]

The Cheyenne people, Cheyenne tribe—I don't know about other tribes—they save that dried-up placenta that comes off, and they keep that, and they make a little case for it. If it's a boy's, it's put in a beaded case, buckskin, the shape of a turtle. Did you ever pick up a turtle? It pees on you! Maybe because boys always pee more than girls. Maybe that's why the turtle shape for boys. No, that's not why! I don't really know!

And if it's a girl, mostly it's a diamond shape, or it can be a triangle—there's no certain shape for girls—it's not a turtle. And if you pierce their ears, why, you have to do it in a ceremony, and do it before they are old enough to grab.

We made blanket cradles for our babies. We'd fasten a blanket

---

2. Compact disc selection 5: Lullaby [1:25]; see also transcription 4, appendix A.

between two ropes with the slack hanging down in the middle for the baby to lie in. And we used to wear T-shaped dress that left seams open for nursing—we could sew up the seams later. We used to wipe our face, wipe the baby's hands with those sleeves. We could hide the baby while it was nursing, but men weren't crazy for your tits like they are now. They took 'em as for baby—not be played with. That was white peoples' introduction: titties.

And you can see how those white girls dress. They're not ashamed! I always say, if their grandmas come back out of the grave and saw how they're dressed—they'd fall right back down. My people, too, they used to wear long dress, but those old ladies, those white women, they used to wear dress down to the ankle— show no part of their leg. These pictures, now—I get ashamed of them. I don't know who they are, but to expose their bodies to everybody, to the whole world, I don't think that was intended before God. I think that we are supposed to have some pride within ourselves in our body, and I don't think God ever intended that kind of exposure for bodies. Men too!

Back when my baby was little, that was the Dust Bowl days. That dirt piled up until you couldn't see the fence posts, they were covered, and they had to push dirt off the road so we could have a road to go back and forth. That dirt would sift into the house, even if you closed the windows. It could make you sick, and if we had babies in the house, we would have to get damp rags and kind of made a shield over our babies.

And I still cover my dishes to keep the dust off. You know, we didn't have cupboards. We had to stack them up on the table, under the table, wherever. My mother used to cover her dishes because a Ponca woman told her the spirits would come and eat out of them if you didn't cover them. Maybe that's how to keep the children out of your dishes—tell them that spooks come and use those spoons.

Back in those hard times people would rather give up the best they have than not give something for visitors. Cheyennes still do. If you see visitors coming, you start putting your pots on, even if it's for coffee. Back in those days, if you have visitors, you go out and pump up fresh water. Otherwise, put your coffeepot on and cook something for your visitor. Visitors, you treat them right, even if they're just there for a while.

Now when I married Horace, his mother wasn't very pleased with me. I don't know what she had against me—I never done nothing to her. But Horace, he was married before, and he said, "That was their choice, it wasn't mine." He said, "You are my choice." He said, "We don't have to live with them, we can live by ourselves." And we did.

I lived in a tent when I first married Horace, there was no home for us. We started off in tent. With Horace, well, we used to take turns singing, he knew some songs that I couldn't sing, and he'd sing. Not very much. Horace wasn't much of a singer—but he could. His brother and dad sat at the drum, but not him, he was kind of a shy guy.

I guess Indians are just shy, they've just always been that way. But white people, oh, they want to show everybody, "This is my wife, this is her!" Everybody knows that's your wife, but still they want everybody to know it. And then when somebody wants to know their financial business, huh! "None of your business. You don't have to know it." Isn't that the way they are?

I didn't care for love stories, I didn't care for movies. But loving my husband, well, that's different than being romantic over a picture, or just over somebody singing. See, Indians don't show their love like white people do. It's kind of private for them.

Horace had a grandson, and we raised him from a baby—that was Clifford. He was born in a tent right beside our house. And we took him for our son, oh, we had a good time with him. And then, I've raised all my own grandchildren in my house at some time—three girls and two boys.

But Horace liked to drink, he liked to be with rough guys, you know. Away from the crowd, that's the kind he was. He enjoyed his drink with his friends until I had to bear down on him. "That's it, that's it! I'm through! I don't want to live that way all the rest of my life. Been married to you for eleven years, and now I'm tired of it, I'm not going to take it no more. I'm quittin'! I'm quittin'!"

So he had to make himself quit. I quit him—I moved away from him three or four times, and he'd come back and get me, and he'd say, "I promise you, I won't drink no more. I won't leave you and Clifford, I'll be with you. I won't leave you no more." I said, "You know, we got things at home you have to take care of."

When we first started making a living, I must have been in my thirties. We couldn't afford to make a big house. But so as far as we could make a one-room house, it was about fourteen by sixteen. But we couldn't finish the porch. And we had a brush arbor that we used all summer. People just lived in those things, they were cool, and we'd wet the ground and it would get hard-packed.

Out there we had a big range, one of those old-time cookstoves. They had a place for hot water where you put water in there and there was a fire on the other side here where you put in wood. The heat from the wood heated the water, and also the oven.

I used to have a lot of chickens and turkeys, and two dogs, Boogie and Popeye. No porch, but a platform in front, and that was my house.

You know, we were raising Horace's grandson Clifford, we were raising him as a son. And we had cattle, and machinery. We used to separate the milk and the cream, but it got to where it wasn't worth fooling with. And that separator, oh, it was work! It had thirty-two cups, and you had to wash every one of them—sterilize them— you had to use hot water to clean or else. And so I got tired of it. We had our separator and we had a tractor, and we had horses out in the country. We lived out there—and 3E was our brand. His name, Horace Little Coyote—all the names end with *e*. So I had it registered down there in Taloga at the county seat—that was our brand, 3E.

So I had to bear down on him, and he had to make himself quit. I had my first husband's initial here on my right hand, and one day I said, "I'm going fix this on my hand." So I went and got a new tattoo put on there, just to erase that initial. So that day when I had that initial changed, I showed my husband Horace, and he said, "Let's go get some tattoos—I'll put your name on my arm, and you put my name on your arm." And so I put his name on my arm, and a new 3E tattoo and a bluebird on my other arm. But now you can't hardly see that 3E tattoo.

During the war, my husband Horace got his army training at Fort Riley. I had to get a passport to go see him—we had to go across that river from Junction City north of Enid. They took my picture.

My eyebrows, I used to pick them with tweezers. I never wore makeup, lipstick or makeup. All I did was put cream on my face and pluck my eyebrows. I didn't wear my wedding ring all the time—I always had my hands in water. I used to use Woodbury cream, something I could afford. I put my hair back there in a bun. I didn't wear my hair down straight—I didn't have much hair. I didn't have big braids, but I used to braid it. And then I'd fix it back like a figure eight in the back.

So I had to go get a picture, and wear it on my clothing, and we'd ride on a bus going across the river, and there was the guard, and I had to show my identification.

We had to get a marriage license when Horace was about to be shipped out. See, back somewhere in the 1930s the government quit recognizing Indian weddings as legal—so we had to get married legally, through paper, black and white. A lot of people witnessed our Indian wedding, but we had to get our Indian marriage legalized so that I could receive the benefits of a wife.

We sneaked off to Oklahoma City to get our marriage license.

We bought the license in that courthouse and we went up to the judge and he married us. I don't know why we sneaked off, we had no reason to hide out. We just didn't want our name in the paper, I guess, but anyway a couple of Horace's relatives went with us. And I think they kind of smelt the rat. I guess they bought the Daily Oklahoman the next morning, and there we were in the paper that we got married. And they used to tell on us, they'd say, "These old people, this old couple sneaked off to get married, and here they are in the paper." You know, in the real fine print, about who got married that day, I guess they looked for it.

All during those four years of World War II, I was the chairman of the Fonda Seiling War Mothers. We had a big celebration when the boys came home. We had bought bonds, and we cashed them. We cashed our bonds, and we bought beef, and all the makings of eatings, and everything else. Oh, then we celebrated! Oh, we celebrated—soberly, too! We had a big powwow.

We did scalp dance, and we danced victory songs, and you don't hear those songs anymore. At that time they were still being sung. But because nobody sings them, after the war was over nobody kept on singing them, we lost them.

Now our Fonda War Mothers Club, that was for war mothers. A war mother does not have to be a mother. It can be any relative, it can be sister, it can be aunt. It's somebody that loves that boy that's in service and wants to join a club. And so that club is a war mothers club.

Nowadays, there's service clubs, but ours was one of the first ones organized, we called it Fonda War Mothers, and later on what you call service club popped up. I don't know where it originated from, but anyway those service clubs got names, but we stayed as Fonda War Mothers even till today.

And the club consists of mothers, like I said, it's the relatives of the boys that was in service. Men were also included in the club, but the mothers, the women, ladies, they had the biggest part. The men, they did the singing for us. And if they wanted to get up and dance with us, when the war mothers were called on to dance and participate, those men would be in on it. If those men had a loved one that was in service, well, they danced with us. But this went on all during the war years, and then after that war was over, we just kind of disbanded since everything quieted down. We just kind of quit getting together anymore.

But now, I notice that they're calling on the service clubs to take part in our Indian social activities or our benefit dances. The sponsors, the ones that have the dance, they want the help of the war mothers service clubs. They want help at the benefit dances—they want us to come, bring food, dance, give away, help out. So, I think it would be a good idea if us war mothers that are still living would reorganize. I think it's an honorable club to represent our boys—the veterans regardless of whether they're black, white, Indian, they're all our boys as war mothers.

We didn't say, that's a white boy, he's not what our club is for— we included everybody that served in our country. We were the war mothers. And you know there's some of us that are church-going people, we prayed for those soldiers. Some war mothers are from different churches, and Native American Church, and they pray for them, too. Like this tipi meeting they have, all night service, they pray for them. A lot of that praying went on.

When the war mothers dance, all stand up together. We had special blankets, they weren't exactly the blanket that you would think of, like a Pendleton blanket—it wasn't that kind. We bought material, maybe it was gabardine, whatever it was, it was the material we could get at that time. The Fonda War Mothers, their color was gold, and our blanket shawls were trimmed with navy blue ribbon. We had a lady, a white lady that knew how to do this machine that would write the name of the boy that was in the service on our blankets. And we wore those when we danced.

The shawls were long, long length, because you couldn't wear it in half like you do a regular shawl because our war mothers shawls had a lot of embroidery work, machine embroidery work in the back of it, so therefore we had no fringe, just that blue ribbon was on the edge. I still have my Fonda War Mothers Club shawl, gold and blue—I think I'm the only one still has their shawl. I remember another group from that time that had white and green. You could recognize the clubs by their colors when they got up and danced.

These clubs started in World War II, but they had them during Korea, Viet Nam, Persian Gulf. Each club had their own song, and the words in them identified the boys that were in the service. Those words identified them as men that went and fought for our country and for us here at home.

Our club had a song. I can still sing the "Fonda War Mothers Song" if I practice it. With this voice that I got! I'm going to practice it a little bit and see if I know all the words that used to go in it. Put it on the recording with this book, and those ladies, those Fonda War Mothers, they'll recognize it. It's kinda hard to remember, it's kinda hard to because we haven't sung it for so long. I sing mostly church music now, and something about Indian church music makes it have a different way of singing.

You can't write it down like they do church songs. Church songs are different than these War Dance, round dance songs, and I have to think now when I recall the "Fonda War Mothers Song." I know the words that go into that song, used to know them, I think if I get the tune, I will know where the words go in.

We're addressing the soldier boys, our boys: "Soldier boys, because we love you, that's why we are organized as a club."

Now, that "Fonda War Mother's Song," it was sung during World War II. A man by the name of John Hill made that song, and he used to say it was a Sioux tone, Sioux tribe tone. And he was part Sioux, and then he put Cheyenne words in there, that's where it came from. That tune, well, any Indian tune belongs to all tribes. But it's just the words that's put in there that makes it different—

it's Cheyenne. John Hill gave it to the Fonda War Mothers and it was given to them as their song—it belongs to the club, Fonda War Mothers.

Maybe somebody would like to catch that tune. I'm singing it like we learned it originally, and if somebody wants to sing it, I wish they would put the words in there where they put the tone of the singing part where there's no words put in. Sometimes they sing a song without the words and then try to put words into it and sometimes they don't put the words in there just right. It skips a beat, I mean it doesn't sound right.

Now, I want that song straightened out. I'd like to see some young folks learn it. Listen and learn it. I mean that I hope that whoever learns this song—which I do hope people will learn it— would be sure and put that music with the words just the way I sang it. This is right, the way I sang it, and I put the words in there right and they'll fit if you sing the words right. If you can talk Cheyenne, you can fit them in. I'd like to see this song straightened out—for people to know it and sing it right.[3]

That's why I stress, whoever learns the "Fonda War Mothers Song," I wish they would learn it just like I sang it, and put the words in there just like I did. Because I'm an old hand at singing that song.

I'm going to tell you about my dream I had during World War II. My son, Woodrow, was in the service; he was in the navy. And this was his fourth time he was to go out on the water, the ocean, and he was close to being discharged.

But in the meantime while he was in there, as a Cheyenne woman I had vowed I was going to make a tipi for my son, to ask the Lord to protect him and bring him back, because he was the only child I had. And when he came back, I had this tipi made, I made it.

---

3. Compact disc selection 6: "Fonda War Mothers Song" [2:25].

Maybe people haven't seen very many tipis that's decorated, anymore, because that's fading out, decorated tipis. But anyway, one night, I can't recall the date and the year I had this dream, I can still remember very vividly how I had this dream.

I seen a tipi, I was there. It was a plain white tipi. I was standing there by that tipi and I seen these American boys—soldiers—they were rushing, they were running, they were running toward this tipi. There wasn't a whole bunch of them—about eight or ten boys.

I said, "Run in here, into that tipi!" It was set up. I said, "Run in here. They can't go in this tipi." I said, "Stand against the tipi and hold your hands up—hold onto them tipi poles and stand as close as you can to that tipi." And I was standing inside at the door. And I heard running, I heard them, somebody, I didn't know whether it was our boys or whether it was Germans.

But I heard them running again. And when they came to this tipi, I was standing there and they looked in. These Germans wouldn't come in the doorway, they just peeked in. And in my dream, our boys were *gone,* they just kind of disappeared. These Germans looked around and they went on. Wasn't a whole lot of them, but it was enough to represent German soldiers in my dream. They went on. I came out, and I saw this wall. My tipi always faces east, that tipi was facing east, and when I came out there was a cement wall. On my left-hand side of the tipi was a cement wall, and one end of it, I would say on the west end, it was crumbling, torn down, and I looked at it, and I said, "I wonder what this was? I wonder what it was?" I looked at that, I noticed that wall, but I didn't know what it was and I was thinking what was it, that was what I was still wondering.

And it wasn't so very long after that, I don't recall, how long that was along there, the ones I told to hide there while I was standing at the door, I said to them, "Come on! Come on out, they can't get you." And then I saw this wall. Like I said, I woke up after I saw the wall. And it wasn't long after that the war was over.

It was after the soldiers all came home, after they all came home, after they all came home, *then* we celebrated.

After the war, my husband and I lived out there in Colorado for a while, just about seven or eight months. We had cattle, ten or twelve. I didn't like it out there—too many people. I'm so used to Oklahoma, so rough and dry and ugly, nothing good about it. I'm just used to this home state. I've seen a lot of good country, and then I want to get home to Oklahoma.

Used to, Horace liked to travel. He'd always save money, go to Montana. In February we'd go to Laredo to see bullfights. Then we got tired of them. One time we were in California, we saw these trick riders, they wanted to take my picture with them, and she put her war bonnet on me—a war bonnet with eagle feathers. They were Sioux, and they were trick riders. My husband took that picture, he snapped it, but the camera belonged to those trick riders.

I like horses, but I don't like to ride them. My sisters used to ride them, my mother used to ride them, race horses, Indian race horses, but not me. My sister was old enough to ride horses, she was born in 1899 or something.

They used to ride horses at these big fairs—at Weatherford, at Cantonment. Cheyenne, Arapaho, they used to have challenges. They didn't wear riding pants, they wore dresses, long dresses. I guess they used to take a cotton blanket.

(Back then we didn't have sheets, I guess we did have thin material, but we didn't know we could make sheets out of it. Thin material was all dress material, and they didn't know muslin, that it could be used for sheets.)

Anyway, they'd wrap their legs with a cotton blanket, tie it or pin it, and make it look like pants. That was their race clothes.

My sister said one time the Arapahos wanted to challenge her as a rider. My sister said, "My horse was just ready to go, and when we heard that gun go off, my horse just took off. We were just going side by side, around that corner, around that first curve, you could hear them holler, hollering. When I came back around that home stretch, this Arapaho girl's horse bucked, just took off of the track, and I won the race." That horse ran right off the track. That was before my time—I just heard about it.

One time I went with Horace to pick peyote, and we went on a truck. I wanted to go, so I went. I don't use it, never did, but I wanted to see where it grew, what it was like, and I wanted to ride in that truck, open—we sat on a truck. Rode to Laredo. The Mexicans told us where there was peyote. And everyone said, "The first one that finds peyote, holler!"

Just a few miles from my house here, on that road to Fonda, Horace was working on a government project bridge—a culvert, like. It collapsed on him June 2, 1955. I cried by myself, but I tried to act brave when people were around. Last time I saw him in the casket, I kissed him and I said, "I'll see you again." And they took me by each arm and led me away from the casket.

I knew I would see him again. Horace worked as a janitor at the church, and he would take me with him to clean the church, and he'd say, "Get up there and sing—I'll work, I want to listen to you sing." So I'd get a hymnbook and turn pages and sing, and he'd work. That's what he wanted me to do. And he come around— about one month before he died, he was baptized.

Lot of girls, I think, they just marry for security, nowadays. I don't think it's true love. Well, I'm glad Virginia found somebody that she is pleased with and loves and she gets along with.

I did some thinking, and this is what I did for Virginia and Neal for their wedding present. I've got this Pendleton blanket that I have used on my bed, and I have covered with it, and I have covered with it out in the cold, taken it to a dance—it's used. But I wanted her to have it. Because I wanted Virginia to remember me by it after I'm gone.

It's going to last her a long time, she'll have it a long time, and I thought, well, this is something I can give her that she'll always think of me when I'm gone when she sees that blanket—she'll think, "It come from her—she's still with me."

If I bought her something new and gave it to her, gold, silver, whatever, it wouldn't be with me—"I just bought it to give to you." But this blanket is something that has been with me, I've worn it, and then I'll be with her after I'm gone. She can have it cleaned, but it's just the thought, you know. I told her not to put it away, but put it where she can use it.

Now this blanket I'm talking about, it's an original, they're old, they're made better than these new ones. I told Virginia she could clean it, but she said, "I don't want to clean it. That will take all the Bertha out of it."

Bertha Little Coyote about age eighteen. *(Collection of Bertha Little Coyote)*

Girls with their legs wrapped for riding horses. (*Photo 13, John Sipe Collection, Western History Collections, University of Oklahoma Library*)

Cantonment School. *(Photo 3, J. P. Hart Collection, Western History Collections, University of Oklahoma Library)*

Indian girls in bullhides, Concho Indian School, 1913. (Photo 92, van Cleave Collection, Western History Collections, University of Oklahoma Library)

Concho Indian School, 1926. The girls' dormitory was brick; the boys' dormitory is in the center. *(Photo 16, Shuck Collection, Western History Collections, University of Oklahoma Library)*

Dust storm, 1930s. *(Photo 72, Corn Historical Society Collection, Western History Collections, University of Oklahoma Library)*

The old stone commissary building at Cantonment, 1931. The only building of the original army installation and government school still standing today. (*Photo 8, J. P. Hart Collection, Western History Collections, University of Oklahoma Library*)

Bertha and her dogs, Boogie and Popeye, in front of her brush arbor kitchen. *(General Conference, Mennonite Church)*

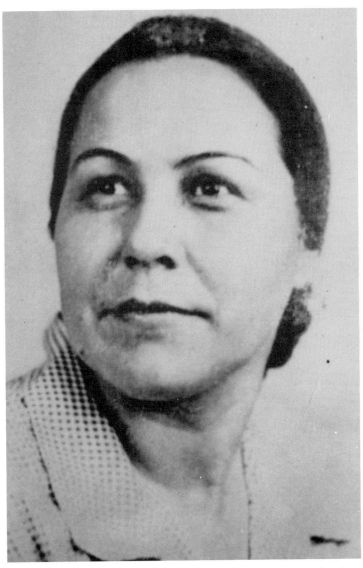

Bertha at age thirty-three; photograph used for her pass to visit her husband, Horace Little Coyote, at Fort Riley, Kansas, 1945. *(Collection of
Bertha Little Coyote)*

Sewing Day at Fonda Church, about 1945. Inez Cloud Chief, Bertha Little Coyote, Mrs. Dan Allrunner and Mrs. Meat display their hand-made quilts. *(General Conference, Mennonite Church)*

Posing with Sioux trick riders at Knotts Berry Farm, California, 1952.
(Photo by Horace Little Coyote)

Bertha demonstrates beading moccasins at the Folklife Festival in Washington, D.C., 1970. *(National Anthropological Archives, Smithsonian Institution)*

Bertha Little Coyote, Community Health Representative, Cheyenne and Arapaho Tribes of Oklahoma, 1972. *(Collection of Bertha Little Coyote)*

Bertha and grandson, Joe, about 1976. *(Collection of Bertha Little Coyote)*

Demonstrating how Cheyenne women carried their babies on their back at Mennonite Church Camp near Seiling, Oklahoma. Bertha with grandson, Joe, 1978. *(General Conference, Mennonite Church)*

Bertha dances at a powwow in Kingfisher, Oklahoma. *(Collection of Bertha Little Coyote)*

Virginia and Bertha dancing at Oklahoma Indian Nations Powwow, Concho, Oklahoma, 1991. *(Photo by Derek Bendure)*

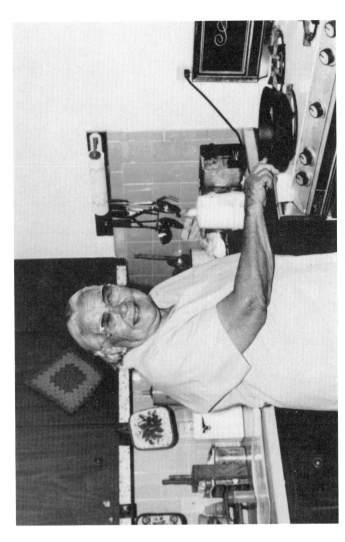

Bertha in her kitchen, Seiling, Oklahoma, 1991. *(Photo by M. J. Ruggles)*

Chapter Four

Dinah Shore Days

In Cheyenne country, Bertha Little Coyote was a singer so reliable, re-spected, and popular that she earned the nickname "Dinah Shore." Bertha tells us the story of being recorded for Indian Records, Inc., in 1969, and in her reminiscences regarding the project we learn about the musical roles of men and women, past and present, around the drum, on the dance floor, and in the late-night song and dance par-ties known as Forty-Nine. (The compact disc contains Bertha's com-mentary about the songs as well as newly remastered editions of those songs.)

Bertha brings a Cheyenne musician's insight into descriptions of song repertoire and the proper uses of songs. She answers questions about how to identify song types and why certain song types earned their names. She describes the phenomenon of lulu—the high-pitched ululation of Cheyenne women, often the intermittent accompaniment of stirring songs honoring a family member. (She also points out the different types and reasons for the "hollering" of men in various settings.)

The recurring theme of giving away reappears as Bertha explains the traditional method of bringing a child into the dance arena. We dis-cover that honor dances for soldiers are held for both men and women as their entrance into or discharge from armed service is formally ob-

served. From Bertha's description of her public commemoration of her son Clifford's fiftieth birthday, we learn that giving away is an integral part of larger public events such as powwows.

In describing her taste in dancing shawls, Bertha gives us clues to the construction, care, and use of these colorful and meaningful garments. This leads to more information about one event at which shawls are worn: benefit dances. A brief explanation of the duties of the "head staff" (those who are invited to take leadership roles at a dance, such as Head Man Dancer, Head Lady Dancer, Head Singer, and so on) and the method of ordering their individual dance and give away events.

How does one join the singers at the drum? Bertha's answers about the nature of the "drum" (that is, the singing group that gathers around the drum) reveal the privileges and responsibilities of singers as well as the varying personalities and talents one can find there. She gives specific information about the male and female melodic lines within ensemble singing of the drum and complains that lack of knowledge of the Cheyenne language can cause mixups in text, causing the group to get "out of tune."

Singing has served Bertha as a survival mechanism, and she asserts that this is the case with many Cheyenne women. Offering a quiet people a way to express their feelings, singing, Bertha believes, can be as effective as prayer as an escape from hurt and loneliness. This is particularly the case with church songs, and although she has never composed a song, she believes her special musical gift is the ability to remember those songs she has learned from others. And the purpose of songs of any kind? Bertha tells us it is to inspire and to uplift the people.

She points out that there are several types of church songs: those in which Cheyenne words have been used with standard Christian hymn tunes (such "How Great Thou Art"), those that are based on traditional Indian melodies, and new melodies that have been made (composed) with Cheyenne texts by composers such as her old friends Belle Rouse and Frances Goose. Men and women compose hymns, but Bertha

maintains that the types of songs heard around the drum are usually
made by men.

Bertha has advice for those who want to sing and shares songs and
experiences from her background as a hymn singer as well as a singer
of traditional Cheyenne repertoire. She explains that song repertoire is
not transmitted by means of "white man's note music" but rather main-
tains its life by being sung. She grieves that some songs are lost in the
oral/aural process, the reason she has dedicated herself to preserving her
memories and songs by means of this book and compact disc.

It's twenty years too late to catch the best in me—singing. But, oh,
I used to be able to sing loud!

About 1969, one day Roy Nightwalker came by and got all of us
and we went down to Fay, to the school, and Oscar Humphreys
recorded us. We made a record, *Seventeen Southern Cheyenne Songs,*
for Indian Records in the town of Fay, Oklahoma—it's owned by
the same man that has the Indian store where people get their
shawl fringe and other things. He recorded us singing—my husband's brother Hailman and his wife Mary, Denny Old Crow, and
Roy Nightwalker. Oscar Humphreys's wife, Nene, she used to call
me "Dinah Shore."[1]

After we sang all these songs, these Scalp Dance songs, these War
Dance Songs, and all them, we run out of songs. The male singers
run out of songs, so we put those Forty-Nine songs in there, those
social dances on there—there's no words in them. Forty-Nine—
that's more like teenagers did—they'd dance all night to them
Forty-Nine songs.

Yes, those Forty-Nine songs—that's more like social dance for
the young people. It's just the beat of the drum, the song, the

---

1. The 1969 recording *Seventeen Southern Cheyenne Songs,* IR 320, is still available from Oscar Humphreys, Indian Records, Inc., Box 47, Fay, Oklahoma
73646, telephone (405) 887-3316.

tune—we know what kind of dance it belongs to. There's no title to it. The only kind of title they have is just Forty-Nine.[2]

If I was at a Forty-Nine singing, I'd be dancing. Like a round dance, but different steps, just one side step, then the other foot, quick, like that.

Women know when to sing the songs. How do they know? Well, that just comes with the song, I guess, I don't know—and not just Forty-Nine, all the other songs, too, we know when to chime in.

Mostly the women dance, the men are singing. They're bunched up, and they sing together and then the women chime in. Women are usually on the outer skirts, you know. But now, they mix, boys and girls mixed. This younger generation they tore it all up.

I don't know when I went to my first Forty-Nine. They didn't become very popular until after my young days. This Forty-Nine came from the south, the Kiowas, you know. It wasn't originally Cheyenne, it come from the Kiowas and the Comanches down there. It's just a social dance. Not religious, just social dance. Sometimes they'd last all night. Sometimes now they break in and start Forty-Nine song at a benefit dance to get those young people in there to dance. They like that, it's their pace.

Down at Fonda Community Hall, we tried to keep them from having Forty-Nine dance. Sometimes it gets too rough. So we tell spooky stories. We tell them stories about sounds of children playing, things like that.

Some spooky things do happen other places, like down at Comargo, south of Seiling. There was this Indian woman a long time ago, and her father forced her to marry. After she died, people could hear her laughing, a laughing ghost. She never did anybody

---

2. Compact disc selection 7: Comments, Forty-Nine Song [2:05] and selection 8: Forty-Nine [2:45]; see also transcription 7, appendix B.

any harm. I don't think spooky things happen at Fonda, but we make them kids think they do.

Some Forty-Nine songs are just chant, but some have a lot of words in them. They have some love words, you know, describing their love, you know how it is, they put words in there. They're getting where they put English words in those Forty-Nine songs.

Now, songs used for round dance—there's a lot of songs used for round dance. They can have the same step, but they have different meaning to us. *Ni zi o zi yo o*—you must come. *Dī iv*—tonight, any night. *Na do zi no gi yo*—I'm gonna be alone. Roy Nightwalker's singing: "You must come, you must come tonight, I'm going to be all alone." She's inviting her boyfriend, I guess. Yeah, "I'm going to be all alone." Round dance songs have the same beat as some other songs, but the words in it tells us where it belongs.[3]

If the man sings a certain chant, you'd know whether it was round dance, or Scalp Dance, or whatever. You don't just go by words, you go by the tune, and by the chant of a song. Then you know where it belongs. The tune and the beat, and the chant syllables. They been around so long that we know them. We don't know who made them up, they're old songs.

Like the Scalp Dance, it belongs to a war, a war party, when you went to Germany, that's where all these songs originated. Now this old song, it originated with World War I. Surely they had songs like this before that, but I never heard them. But this song means, "German, if you turn, if you run back, would you be a man? Would you be considered a man?" It's kind of sarcastic, I guess.[4]

3. Compact disc selection 9: Comments, Round Dance Song [3:00] and selection 10: Round Dance Song, "You Must Come Tonight" [1:46]; see also transcription 8, appendix B.
4. Compact disc selection 11: Comments, Scalp Dance Song [2:21] and selection 12: Scalp Dance, "If You Turn, Would You Be Considered a Man?" [1:14]; see also transcription 9, appendix B.

The other old song has two verses. The first verse was for the German, and the next verse was for the Japanese. It says, like, "German, pert near turned to coyote—he fled, disappeared—he turned his back and disappeared. Running, you know, he fled, turned and fled, disappeared. And the same thing, Japanese. *O da khī ni,* Japanese. These Germans, we describe them "red white man"—*ma i vi ho.* Guess they have reddish skin, or whatever, that's the way they look.

Yes, he knows somebody's after him, and he disappeared. Now that other song said, if you turn, what kind of man can you be? This song is about how he turned.[5]

When they dance Scalp Dance, they always dance with a scalp. They used to do a scalp, they'd tie it on a pole, and then they'd do Scalp Dance with the pole. I've seen women dance it. I don't know about the men. I dance, but I never did Scalp Dance. If somebody wants to dance it, you can dance it. But I never just wanted to dance with a pole, a stick.

Scalp Dance, it's for anybody who wants to dance. And there's lots of participants, you know, that are so glad that their boys and menfolks came home that they dance, they're going to get out there and take part. Whipped! They're whipped, we whipped them, that's what it means. Got their scalps! Oh, they lulu! Yeah, you see a lot of lulu.

Now this lulu—very few know how to lulu—not every Indian woman knows how to lulu. It just comes to some who know how to lulu—natural. My mother used to try to teach me but I couldn't learn it. I said, "That's natural, anybody can lulu. It just comes natural with some of them."

5. Compact disc selection 13: Comments, Scalp Dance Text [3:10] and selection 14: Scalp Dance, "He Fled Like a Coyote" [1:54]; see also transcription 10, appendix B.

The way you do it is with your tongue and your voice some way, I don't know how it's done. Look at somebody that lulus. Tiny, her daughter always lulus. Part white, you know, but she can sure lulu.

Yuyu—what do they call it, you know, they have them kind of sounds? It reminds me, during that war across there when they was fighting, you know, that Schwartzkopf, he was that big shot there, and they whipped that nation—that mean guy, Saddam Hussein. And they released one group or tribe of people from this other— that Saddam Hussein. You know, he was a cross, mean-looking guy. Anyway, when those men were released, we could see it on TV, and those women lulu. They had on black, and I said, "Hey, the women lulu! I guess they do lulu!"

And so many people heard them lulu like we do. Victory. Gladness. And I thought maybe Indians were the only ones. Makes you wonder, where did it come from, lulu? Did Indians come from back across there in the Middle East or did they just scatter?

Now lulu, if you can get it out loud enough, they hear you, that's lulu. The loudness is important—so somebody can hear you. To know that you're glad—a mood, maybe. Anybody can lulu if they want to and can—it's how you feel. You can lulu when there's grieving, when you see the casket going down. It's not all happiness, it's grieving, too. It has lot of meaning, lulu. It expresses your feelings. And we understand it.

It's like a man, you know, he has a way of hollering, he don't lulu, he holler, he got that war whoop, they call it. A man's got his own way of holler. And sometimes at the graveside he'll do that to say, "Goodbye, farewell." It can be a sad sound, or it can be a victory or a happy sound.

Wherever it's applied, that's what it is. Sometimes if you know why they lulu, if it's for sad occasion, it just makes you feel so sad. It just makes a funeral just so much sadder, I would say. And when it's a happy time and somebody lulus, it just makes it more lively.

Women, the only thing they got is lulu. Men, they have different ways of hollering, you know, sometimes an individual has his own way. But women have lulu, and they sound different from each other, but you know, it's a lulu. Maybe somebody's got a voice that they can't sing any higher. It's according to how you use your voice. Some Indian women, you know, they don't have high voices.

Now, you have to get it out loud enough where they can hear you. You can tell by the sound, the sound of it. Some of it sounds *real,* just the sound was like some that can carry a tune real pretty and make a song real pretty and inspire somebody the way somebody would sing it, you know. And sometimes lulu don't effect nobody.

Now War Dance, you know, where they jump around—feather dance. There's a difference between war songs and War Dance songs—there's no words in War Dance songs. It's action—and chant only.[6]

Now this is a War Dance song—no words. Those others got words in them, they are war songs. But these War Dance songs, no words in them.

Those war songs, Scalp Dance songs, you dance around, like for round dance, or Forty-Nine. That's where you use those war songs. But this one is a War Dance song.

Now, when you go to a community benefit dance and they play a War Dance song, that's when everybody gets up and walks around. Anybody can dance it, it's no contest. There are no words in it. War Dance songs, that's the only name they have for this War Dance, even if it's fancy, you know, it's War Dance. Then there's other songs that are war songs or Scalp Dance songs. They have words—messages in them. But War Dance, I don't know why they

6. Compact disc selection 15: Comments, War Dance Song [2:19] and selection 16: War Dance Song [2:01]; see also transcription selection 11, appendix B.

are called War Dance, they're just action, fancy dancers dance to them. And at benefit dances, we dance to them, walking around.

Dances like they have now at Fonda, when I was a child, they didn't have them. What we call a benefit dance now was not known as a benefit dance. We had the kind of dance where some individual wanted to honor a relative, son or daughter, during the gathering of a dance. They wanted to honor this person by having a giveaway dance for them, and that's the way they gave away. Honor dances, they were called, and they would have a giveaway after. Head Man Dancer, Head Lady Dancer at benefit dances—they didn't have them like that until recent years.

I'm getting ready to go to a dance for a girl that was in service and she's through with everything—her training, everything—discharged, I guess. I have to make some corn soup and frybread for that dance. I don't like to use anything but Crisco when I make frybread. The government commodities shortening is half lard and half vegetable oil, I think. It's good to make pie crust with.

So this girl's aunt is putting this dance on to honor her. It's a benefit dance—that's what they call it now. Now, what they call pow-wows today are similar to when I was young. When I was twelve, thirteen years old, I started going to dances—powwows.

There's a way people do now when it's the first time a child is to dance. When a child that is less than a teenager is brought out by his parents to be initiated into Indian dancing, the announcer, the emcee, announces that he is to be initiated as a dancer. Girl or boy. So the family and other people, they'll get out and, when the drum starts singing, the child will start dancing with his father and mother with all the friends and relatives dancing behind, all around the arena. And when they get through dancing they have their gifts by the announcer's stand and they give away for him and that way he is initiated into the dancing circle. It's an old tradition and some people like to do that—it's a kind of love thing, they want to show people how much they love their child. They give away blankets, possibly a horse (but we don't usually have ponies anymore), dress material, money. Don't make any difference, boy or girl, six years old or so—as long as he's able to dance, wants to dance.

I couldn't afford to do it for my kids. They got out and danced when they wanted to. It's not a necessity to give away, but some people that's got pride in their family, or something—they do it.

Now, in July of 1995, it was my son Clifford's fiftieth birthday. There was a powwow in Seiling, and I gave away for him. There was a feed—I made two briskets and a great big pan of frybread. I asked for a special, and the emcee announced it, and we did a War Dance and Gourd Dance, and Clifford, he almost cried. And I said to him, "Be happy! I'm happy that you lived to be fifty years old."

When I learned to drape that shawl on my shoulders, I guess that's when I learned to dance. My mother gave me my first shawl, it wasn't fancy work. There were no decorations shawls when I was a young girl. But now they decorate them. I like patch decorations—appliques. Patches look more Indian than floral designs, but I sure do love flowers. On a shawl, I don't like red with white fringe, I like red with red or red with black. I wouldn't put white fringe on a red shawl. White designs on red look nice if it's close together and the fringe is thick, about a half inch apart, but I see so many scattered three-fourths or one inch apart. And they're bringing back that flip fringe, fringe made of ribbons.

I got so upset when I lost my good shawl—I had it for four or five years, a white one with red fringe and a rose design on it. I was going to be buried in it. It was nice material that didn't slide, and the rose design was cut out, I think it was bought, small roses on a vine, no longer than three inches wide, sewn on with fine zigzag, a lot of work. I really prized it, the way it was made. I meant to put new fringe on it and have it cleaned. I been telling these people, if you ever see this shawl somewhere, let me know. That's the way it is with Indians, there's one shawl or blanket that they really like.

I bought some fabric to make some shawls, I've got to do a give-away at that dance coming up. I bought some purple fabric and some dark pink fabric, polyester gabardine, I'm going to fringe it and put some designs on it.

What I do after I finish a shawl, I put it together and press it even, then I've got the fold up here, then I make a little stitching across, and that way it don't come apart when you put it on. Do that to your shawl, just a little seam across there. You don't get out there and dance without a shawl on you unless you are half drunk. But drunk people get pulled out of the ring real quick.

Now benefit dances can be expensive. You see somebody you want to help, and there goes another dollar. If you are called upon to help out at a dance, head staff, you have go up during the signups so that they can tabulate your name. Somebody keeps up with who gives away first, second, third. First you dance, then you give away. Third place can be first if first and second place aren't signed up.

You ask, is there any special routine or whatever for the girls to sit, or the ladies to sit behind the drum at a powwow or a dance? No, there isn't. If you want to sing with the men, that's your privilege to get out there and sing with them. And they like that. All of us Indians like to hear male voices and female voices, that makes a sound of the Indian music better.

No, there's no ritual for anybody to get out there and sing with the men. Now some of them, lately, with little girls, sometimes it's just that somebody wants to get a little more money so they put a chair out there for their little granddaughter to get money. They'll get a dollar when that Head Singer shares out the money dollar by dollar from the giveaways or shawl auctions to each person sitting around the drum.

You don't have to know every song to sit behind the drum, and not everyone wants to sing out loud, you know. You know, mostly, Indian women they're kind of quiet about their music. There are some that like to sing out, like me. I like to sing out. And that's the way it is, if you want to sing, you take your chair up there and sit with the men and sing with them. You don't make a mistake—they lead, you follow. The males, you just kind of sing along with what they do—the women start at their time. It's the music, I don't know how to explain, but there's a certain time for them to start with the male.

They don't get mixed up and sing in the male part but when they put words in there, they do get mixed up, even the men. If there's somebody that's trying to put words in there that does not speak good Cheyenne, then they get out of tune, and they get others out of tune.

I used to sit at the drum—any drum, I could sing with them, because I liked to sing. I used to could sing—I never thought my voice would give out.

I think I was just born to be a singer. I always liked to sing any kind of Indian music I pick up, and church music, religious music. I suppose Indians are so uplifted by songs because an Indian doesn't speak out how they feel. They wouldn't tell you how they felt, you know, or not very many of them will tell you, so easily, "This is the way I just feel." Instead, they keep it all to themself, how they feel.

I've talked with women who say, you know, they get so lonely they just think there's no escape. They pray, but it seems like that there's no escape, and then they sing.

I love to sing. Singing is part of my life, I would say, because also it makes me happy to sing. When I'm sad, if I don't feel like singing, I sing anyway, you know, and pretty soon I'm relieved of a lot of what I'm worrying about. And not just to sing the song by itself, but sing and think prayerfully that I'm gonna forget what's worrying me. And when I hear something bad and I don't want to remember it, I sing a church song.

There's different kinds of Indian songs and I like to sing those songs. Round dance, War Dance, whatever the activity is, there's a song for it.

I sing in church more now, and I enjoy singing church songs—white or Indian church songs. We Cheyennes have some Christian people who made songs inspired by the spirit, maybe in a dream, and they brought these songs out. And they sing them, and that's how they come to us.

Those inspired church songs, they were pretty near gone for a while, nobody cared to learn them. Some wanted white music, you know. And they were pretty near gone until somebody was led of the spirit to bring out these Indian church songs. There was a lady from Clinton, Oklahoma, her name was Belle Rouse and another one was Frances Goose. They came to me one time.

"We want you to learn these songs," they said.

"Why me?" I said.

They wanted me to learn them. So I heard them once or twice but they stuck with me, the songs that they sang. And there's others that composed these Indian church songs—I've learned them from Paul Littleman, Harvey White Shield, and I love to sing those church songs.

And I helped out with gathering those songs together. Back in 1974, there was a Cheyenne Christian leaders meeting, and folks from Montana and Oklahoma got together to put these songs into a book. They kept going with that, and I helped with the brown book *Tsese-Ma'heone-Nemeotôtse* which is "Cheyenne spiritual songs." And that book is still used today.

I love to sing those church songs, but I never composed them. Maybe I wasn't smart enough to compose a song. But I love to sing the ones that I know, that I picked up. No favorite. I like to sing any of them. There's quite a few.

Some have got an Indian tune, made by an Indian. And some have English tunes, and we Cheyennes put Indian words in them. Like "Amazing Grace"—we put Indian words in that and there's others, you know. We put Indian words in that. And "How Great Thou Art"—we use that chorus.[7]

English songs, white songs, they have notes, you know. White man's note music. But Indian music does not have notes—it's kind of a chant. Indian songs don't have notes like the English ones, but we do put Indian words with some English songs.

There's old songs, yes, old melodies from Indian songs that are hymns now. Nobody would take an old Indian song like a War Dance song or mourning song and make it into a Christian song. But you know, there's one church song, only one I can think of, that I always thought was taken from a peyote song. Them people way back there, you know, they didn't know English tunes, but spiritually they were given these songs to sing, maybe in a dream or whatever, and they brought them out and they sang them, and that's where we learned a lot of these songs. These tunes, they're a little bit different. Well, I don't know anything about music, but it's nothing like English.

Anyway, there's one song that's got that kind of tune, that kind of beat, of a peyote song to it. And that's the only one that I would say, "That! That's a peyote tune!" You know, the beat of that peyote drum is a little faster than what you would say is church music, you know. But this song I'm talking about, the beat of it, would you say the rhythm of it? It always says to me, where it came from was from this peyote song. I wonder if anybody could place this song, and know that it was a peyote song. But that's what I always say: somebody put words to that and made it a church song. The words mean "Jesus, look now on us! Have mercy! Be merciful!"[8]

I participated in a peyote meeting only one time—back when

7. Compact disc selection 17: Hymn, "How Great Thou Art" [:57]
8. Compact disc selection 18: Hymn, "Jesus, Venave'hoomemeno" (Jesus, look now on us) [2:05]; see also transcription 12 (Hymn 122), appendix C.

that appendix attack came on me and my mother put up a prayer meeting night. They have pretty music in those meetings. They have music that belongs to that religion, their peyote religion. But this song I sang just now, I think somebody put Christian church words in that peyote religion song.

Mostly men know those peyote songs. Well, women sing along if they want to, but usually they don't. It's mostly the men sing them. That peyote religion, it's all over the nation, and most of the tribes, they make up their songs, just like any other song. I never heard about women making a peyote song—they don't make peyote songs, always the men.

And War Dance songs, well, same way. The men make them. But these church songs, well, there's women involved. Lots of women make these Christian church songs. Frances Goose and Belle Rouse, they used to go around together. And they practiced making up songs, I guess. Belle was telling me that she was compelled through the spirit to make songs, and she said they come to her. She studied music when she went to school at Chilocco Indian School. I guess that anybody that wants to make a song could make a song.

One thing I get asked to do is sing church songs at the graveside, like "This World Is Not My Home." They put Cheyenne words in that English tune. And we put Indian words to "In the Sweet By and By."

We try to teach these church songs so that people that sing them will be inspired. Indians have always been inspired by songs. Through a song, no matter how a person mourns or how lonesome they are, if they sing a song they get uplifted. Songs, Indian songs, Indian tunes, or church songs—they uplift the people.

And when an elder gets up to pray, sometimes they will cry. Why? Spirit hits you! I do it, too. When I'm asked to pray, it's a burden. To me it's a burden to pray for people. A heavy burden, because you're praying for all kinds of people. You don't know who is a believer and who isn't a believer. And all that burden is put upon you—all that is on you when you pray for all of them. Sometimes it's kind of hard to find words to pray to feel like you're praying for everybody, especially when you are praying in Indian, you know. There's so much to pray.

Now, to be a good singer, you have to want to sing. And I think its the same way with the English singers, you're going to have to want to sing to really sing. If I saw a singer smoking, I would tell her to quit—but it wouldn't do any good. But I would tell her— I would. That smoking, it affects your throat.

I tried smoking, way back in my thirties, forties, somewhere there. Everybody was smoking, and I thought, well, let me try it. I knew how to roll them. I used to take paper and roll Bull Durham for my mother. And I tried it, and I smoked for about three or four months and I didn't like it. Too much bother. I quit it. I didn't smoke for a year. Then I smoked some from time to time, two or three different times I tried it. It just wasn't for me.

I used to have real clear throat, but now I got thyroid problems, that's why one side of my neck its bigger than the other side. I asked my doctor, "Why is my throat bigger on this side?" and he said, "That's caused from your thyroid." And I have to take thyroid medicine every day. That thyroid has affected my voice—I used to have a real clear voice. Now, I don't have a cold, but I sound like it. And a month or so ago, my heart was doing double beat, and I laid real still, and then I couldn't hardly breathe. But I got up and I walked into this room, and I thought, "Bertha, when you feel faint, grab that phone and say, Operator! I need 911!"

But ever since that time, there's something that sounds like I got a cold in my throat, and I don't got a cold. I tried some different kind of cough drops like those singers around the drum use—but they don't clear it. Usually for a cold I gargle with vinegar and water or pickle water—it won't hurt you to swallow it. Maybe I'll always have this kind of voice. Hopefully not, I hope it clears out, but I think it's from that thyroid.

I don't have the voice any more to sing out loud like you do with the Indian songs in a crowd. Of course you don't sing alone—you sing with the men at the drum, and the men sing along. But I don't have that strong voice anymore. So I sing mostly church songs in the church and at funerals. I'm called upon a lot of times to sing at a funeral. Not by myself of course. I take two or three others along to sing, and anyone else that wants to help us sing at a funeral or whatever the occasion may be.

I do have a high voice. I just always take it for granted that that's how God created me, to have a voice like that. There's a song I sing real high:

Red white man,
Where can you run?
Where can you hide?
God is with me.

That song is high. It's high because men sing it more than women. Songs are for anybody that wants to sing. But songs, even though anybody can sing songs, have their place, where they are to be sung. Like War Dance, round dance, Gourd Dance, Ghost Dance. Of course I don't know Ghost Dance. I don't think my mother did, either, or even before that, but Cheyennes had Ghost Dance. But I never heard of anybody still believing in Ghost Dance.

Anyway, I used to hear this song, World War I, and I also heard it in World War II. Of course, there are a number of songs that we're losing because we don't keep singing them. We're losing them. I'm sorry for that.[9]

Now, to Indian people, music just comes. There's no written tune, no written music like whites have music—notes, and bars,

9. Compact disc selection 19: War Song, "God Is With Me" [2:55]; see also transcription 5, appendix A.

sharps, flats, and whatever—it's nothing like that. We don't write it down, the way we sing. But white notes, with Indian words in it, well, we have church music where they have put notes in there and some places they fit, some places they don't.

But this book is to help people understand, white people, Indian people, any people. Like I say, I don't mind telling white people, because how are they going to learn to know me? How are they going to respect my way? Virginia includes note music for some songs in this book for white people to see, but this Indian music—dancing music, whatever, I have never known any Cheyenne to put notes, white music notes, to try to sing these Indian songs. To Indians, music just comes.

Chapter Five

The Lord, the Tribe, and the Mennonite Church

In spite of the forbidding front Bertha put up when I first visited her, she is, by her own admission, tender-hearted and ready to give her friendship on an equal-opportunity basis. She doesn't claim to be an expert on all tribes, but enjoys teaching about Cheyenne ways because she believes this generates respect for her people. For example, she enjoys demonstrating the colorful and descriptive nature of the Cheyenne language and is quick to point out that there are no curse words in Cheyenne. She does not think that she expresses herself as well in English as she does in her native language, but those who do not speak Cheyenne are fortunate that Bertha is committed to sharing her memories with us in a way that we can understand.

Bertha has demonstrated hand arts and inspected historic Cheyenne beadwork at the Smithsonian and enjoyed other trips with Cheyenne elders. She also traveled to out-of-state training sessions for her work as a Community Health Representative. As a CHR, Bertha worked in the tribal health program, acting in a triage capacity, directing tribal members to appropriate care providers, giving rides to the doctor, singing hymns along the way.

Bertha's commitment to a Christian way of life does not preclude her support of tribal religious ceremonies such as the annual Sun Dance.

She respects the ceremonial ways of the Cheyenne people and is always on hand to support them with her voice and prayers.

The Mennonite Church has offered Bertha opportunities to be a cross-cultural communicator, and she is particularly proud of a camp meeting in Seiling, where she demonstrated to German and other non-Indian Mennonites various aspects of Cheyenne tradition—yet another type of giving away.

As a Christian and a Mennonite, Bertha has given a lot of thought to various issues such as baptism, the nature of a heavenly reward, and the day-to-day help that her beliefs provide. She considers Christianity (and boarding school) to have been her deliverance from an unhealthy upbringing by alcoholic parents, and she wishes that all people would live in peace in the realization of one kinship under God.

I got a lot of friends, white, Indian, any race, they talk to me, I talk to them. Even children, two or three people have taken me for a mother. Maybe more! And I've got a brother, Bernard, and I got sister Rose, who took me for a sister after her sister died. I've got friends, relatives, and friends who want to be relatives with me. Why? It's because I got Jesus in my heart, and Jesus shows out. The spirit shows out that I believe in God. I think that shows out, and I think that's why people want to be my friend. They see something in my life.

I don't mind if people ask me questions about my tribe, Indian, Cheyenne, I don't know about other tribes. They've got their own beliefs, everything. Every tribe, every Indian tribe has their own beliefs. But I don't mind telling white people, because how are they going to learn, to know me? How are they going to respect my way if I don't let them know about myself, about my tribe? That's the way I feel about it. I'm not afraid to tell them, so if they ask me something, I tell them.

Maybe what I tell them seems strange and odd and they think that we're creatures or something. But if we don't speak up and let them know that we do know about things. Like our language—we have a different way of describing things. We don't say "hog" or "pig." There ain't no word in "hog"—that's English! So we have to describe that animal as "sharp-nose dog." We know what a dog is, and when our people saw hog, well, hog or pig, all the same, they called it "sharp-nose dog."

Cheyennes are sure reverent with dogs. I have a little Chihuahua named Tomi. I didn't know that a dog could be such a comfort to a lonely person—I didn't know he could be so much company. And he takes care of the house when I'm gone. One time somebody asked me for him, and I said, "That's not my dog, he's my little boy!"

There is a story about a dog saving Cheyennes—directed them out of a storm. That's why the dog came. Pretty near every Indian home used to have a dog, but now they don't because these white people in town won't let you let your dog run loose.

Now coffee, in Cheyenne, that's "black soup." Onions, that's "skunk balls." And oatmeal is "slobbering gravy" or "dirtymouth gravy." Commodity oatmeal—I like it. I like it better than Quaker. You know, I like cold oatmeal. I'll put a little milk in there, if I want a snack. The oatmeal, that's my snack. That's silly, but I like it.

I speak English and I speak Cheyenne, and I read it, too. Well, most of the elderly Cheyennes speak it, and some of the younger ones. Not the real young, but like my children, they know how to talk. The language is hard to teach to children today. "Aw, it's too hard to learn!" they say. But we do give the children Indian names, whether they are ever called by their Indian names.

I myself speak Cheyenne a lot. These older ones can understand me. But the younger ones, nah, they don't want to learn it. Some, I guess they understand a little, you can teach them, but it's too hard, they say. You have to teach them when they're little to get that Cheyenne sound. Like I talked Indian to my boys when they were little, but I talked more English to my son Clifford than I did

Indian. His other grandma talked Indian to him, too, but he made mistakes because both of us didn't talk Cheyenne to him all the time. It was easier to get after him in English. That's how I'd correct him when he was little—in English.

I learned Cheyenne from my mother. This man my mother married, Black Beard, he couldn't speak English, he never had no schooling. So from him my mother learned to talk Cheyenne fluently, I guess.

I don't use white man's cusswords, but I can use Indian dirty language. Seeing's we don't have cussing words in Indian—no tribe that I know of has cussing words, to use God's name in vain. When we want to say something, cuss something, say something dirty, then we use dirty words. That is, using dirty words from your body, not putting God's name in it. Or use white man cusswords. But no Indian—no tribe I ever hear of—takes God's name in vain.

Of course, most of the time I talk easily, but when anybody asks me a question about something, I have to think how I'm going to answer that in English. But in Indian, I could tell you right off how I feel.

Now when I pray, I pray in Cheyenne. I pray in Indian because I feel that God gave me the Cheyenne language to speak, to converse with Him. I always say, "He gave me the Cheyenne language, and I feel free when I pray in my Cheyenne language." I feel that it's coming from my heart. I pray from my heart, I don't have to think what I'm going to say. It just naturally comes out because it's from my heart. And I know what I'm praying about and for, asking for His forgiveness or His help, or whatever, and blessings on the food.

With English, I always feel like I don't know enough of it to put it into words that would be appropriate for my asking to God for the needs of my Cheyenne people, or anything I really feel like I want to say. I speak English, but when I go to praying in English, I have to think, "Am I saying the right word?" As I pray along in

English I have to think of the words I'm going to use, and they automatically come out. But the words do not come as freely as when I pray in Indian, cause I guess I'm used to praying in Indian and I can just pray right on. But in English, sometimes I have to stop and repeat myself, what I really mean.

It's like I say, I didn't master it—I didn't master this foreign language we had to learn, this English. I don't know too much about all the parts, I don't speak it fluently. I have to think what I want to say to you to make it sound right. Most white people don't know I'm always thinking, "How am I going to use this English word?"

But I don't mind people asking me questions. My big mouth has gotten me lots of places. Back in the seventies I went to Washington, D.C. A lady from Indian Affairs came out to Oklahoma who wanted someone to represent the Cheyenne Plains Indians at Washington at the Folklife Festival. So I drove some Cheyenne people down to the University of Oklahoma at Norman to meet her. I was working for the tribe and I used to give rides at the time. And that lady said, "Bertha, it's you I want to take." And I said, "Why didn't you tell me in the first place, I wouldn't have had to make this trip down."

So, I got to go from June 20 through the fourth of July. They put up this big top, this tent, in front of the Smithsonian. I sat there and did beadwork. We stayed in the nearby college and they had guards—they guarded us everywhere we went—even when we ate in the Smithsonian. They had made little arbors for us, shades for us. All the artisans had little booths. There was a big crowd there, and we had to be guarded.

And they took us to a show—there were Greeks and people of different nationalities, and they danced for us. Those Greeks wanted the Indians to sing and dance for them, too. So we danced and then the Greeks danced—oh, they can dance! I enjoyed it. And the group of black people from Alabama or Mississippi or somewhere—oh, they can sing! I just loved that! We'd be waiting for the buses and they'd start singing, and, oh, the harmony. There was a kind of an elderly man, I'd say he was in his early sixties, and he was the leader, and oh, he could sing—I never heard such music. They could sing!

And I roomed with one of those young black girls, and she was so sweet—she was my roommate. And when I'd go take a shower, she'd have my bed laid out, she'd have my shoes laid out. I felt like she must have that instinct of taking care of older people. And when I was leaving, all the little beadwork that I had, I gave to her, and she just grabbed it and she just loved it. I just loved her and enjoyed the few days I was there with her in Washington.

While I was there somebody took a picture of me beading, and they sent me the picture, and the postmaster in Seiling, Mrs. Lucille Sanders, said, "Can I take it?" And she took it to the *Dewey County News* and it was all written up. I was making moccasins—I had finished one, and I was beading the other one. In the picture you can see the top of one, not finished. And beside it, that's my bead can with my beads in it.

But I laid this moccasin there to show—it was one that I took up there to wear. I finished a new pair while I was there and I sold them right there to the Smithsonian. They bought them, and the man that was taking care of that Indian part of that Folklife Festival, they bought them for him to wear because we were going to have powwow and they wanted him to lead that powwow parade right there on the lawn.

The last time I went to Washington was June 1994. I went to see about some old Cheyenne beadwork. And on the airplane the pilot said, "We're going up higher, above the clouds." I was sitting by the window, and pretty soon I couldn't see anything, and that scared me. I said, "Don't put me on a plane again—that's the last one."

So I got to fly to Washington—not at my expense—my big mouth got me there. My big mouth, my knowledge of old things.

Somebody else sponsored it, and asked me to go. When I was there the first time, we stayed close to the Smithsonian, and we saw a lot of exhibits, even Cheyenne—they had a tipi and everything. Camp of a Cheyenne—Cheyenne camp, it said. A tipi, and I've made those tipis—the ones that have decorations on them, I've made that kind.

I've made four tipis, all at different times, but altogether four, and if anybody doesn't believe me, I say, Mary Little Coyote, my sister-in-law, she's still alive, she knows it. That's my proof.

Anyway I recognize this Cheyenne tipi up there. It was the real thing, the way we made Cheyenne tipis. And when I went up there this time to identify beadwork for the Smithsonian, I didn't see that tipi. We went up there last summer, but that exhibit was gone, I don't know what they did with it. They didn't have as good an exhibit as they used to have.

Let's see, I've been to Washington, and Alabama, and over here in Arkansas. And down that way, to Old Mexico, and north, to Montana. I never been to Canada—I had a chance to go, a church group went up there two or three years ago, and I said, "Nah, it's too cold up there, too long a ride." So I didn't go, but I been to the West Coast: California, been to Arizona powwows, Albuquerque, I been lot of places. Maybe eight times I've been on airplane, out and back, that'd be sixteen flights. But I'm through—I'm not gonna fly anymore. I'm afraid of it.

I've been to Taos several times. I was out there again about two years ago this coming September. The elderly, we went out there on a van. We raised money and then the tribe let us use a van so we went out there. It didn't cost us anything, because the tribe let us sell raffle tickets for baskets of groceries, and people would donate items for the basket, or a shawl. And that's the way we raised our money over eight or nine months, and then the tribe gave us some money.

It was just a one-day trip out there, and the place where we stayed wasn't right in town, it was out of town. We stayed near Taos two nights. We fed ourselves, paid for our food. We went to the village, and if any of us wanted to sell any items we put a price tag on them. For ten dollars fee we all shared this one table, this booth. It was kind of a large booth where we could sit and have our display: shawls, moccasin work, anything we had to sell. There were tourists watching. But every item had a price, the name was on there whose item it was. If there was two of a kind, then we'd write the name down and how much they sold that item for.

And the people, they were just thick, and you could tell they were rich people that come out to see Taos, it was kind of a tourist place. You could tell they were tourists the way they would shell out their money. There were booths, booths, booths, booths, booths!

That's a different kind of country, out west, different kind of scenery, but I don't think that's a place I want to be. When I took my Community Health Representative training in Tucson, back in 1969, I flew out there, stayed out there a month. I learned first aid, and they trained us about abuse of alcohol and drugs at the University of Utah—"Alcoholism and Drug Dependencies." And I went down to the University of Oklahoma for training, too. That was all for CHR, Community Health Representative.

As CHR, I had to go around and visit the families and see housewives, you know, see if they needed help—get them to a hospital doctor—direct them where they could get help. Minor things, we were taught, like if somebody got burnt with hot soup, we learned to take care of that, but we couldn't give no kind of medicine. "What do you need?" Write it down, then we'd take 'em to a doctor or they'd get notice to come in. Indians couldn't go over to city hospitals unless the government doctor from Clinton said okay. Transport. I did more transporting than doctoring. And for this I made $322 every two weeks and twenty-five cents per mile.

I drove all over the area of Seiling, Canton, and Longdale. I used to have an El Camino, and my little El Camino used to fit right into the wrecky cars. It was an older model, but it used to run good. And then I used to have a Chevy. I've had several cars, but I enjoyed that El Camino.

And whenever I used to drive, whenever I was traveling alone, I used to sing them, sing church songs. I just hear them and I learn them. Like I said, I never composed any of them. It was people that worked in the church, and even what you call lay people? I never could make a song. But I can sing them after I hear them.

I became a Christian when I was twelve years old—1925. It was in the Mennonite Church. That's the only missionaries we had that took interest to teach us the Bible, and later on others came.

I do have respect for my Indian way, the way my people want to go, the way they do. I respect it. Like Sun Dance. Some things I don't know and I don't ask. But my way is the Bible, church. My people don't throw that up to me. They don't say, "You're a Christian!" They don't say that to me. And I join in the singing out there at our ceremonies, and I support it. You don't have to believe Indian religion, but you can respect, and the Bible says respect.

But I think here at my home people see the Bible, they hear me pray, they see that I go to church and it's got to rub off onto them someway, somehow. I pray at powwows, and these benefit dances, I don't know how many times I pray for these dinners. We don't know how we can lead some people. But I don't preach to them, I just mention it sometimes that they should turn their ways.

Those Mennonites are German, and we used to go over there to Kansas to visit. And I said, "This time, why don't you come over and camp with us?" So they did that one year—a cross-culture camp. And I was showing those young people, talking to them, and I said, "We used to carry our babies on our back." I was demonstrating to them—and I called my grandson Joe. I said, "Come here!" and I said to them, "I'll show you how we used to put that kid on a blanket like that, and bring the blanket up." I laughed! I was showing them how. My grandson Joe, he must have been about five years old—that was about 1978. We camped out twelve miles east of Seiling.

I've been baptized twice, once with sprinkle, the way the Mennonites believe, but I had the feeling that I needed immersion. I'm not a perfect woman, I've made a lot of mistakes, I'm sinful, and I just felt like I haven't been that close to God. I holler for him when I get in a mess, when I get in trouble, "God, help me!" And he does answer, but to really follow him close and his teaching, I didn't. And I got this feeling around 1990 that I'm getting up there, I'm getting up there in years. I need to straighten my life out, I need to get closer to my belief—God, Jesus, Holy Spirit—I need to get straightened out with them, straighten out my life with them. And I want to reach heaven, too, because I been poor, you might say, pretty near homeless here on earth. But who wants to live that way? I don't want to live that way.

I don't want to know what is said in the Bible about destruction and all this misery if you don't prepare for your home in heaven. I believe that, because I read it and I hear it, but I don't want that. I think I've had enough miserable life here on earth, that I want to prepare to meet my God where it's a beautiful place. I love flowers, I just love flowers, and I say, I want to shake hands with Jesus—I want to see him and shake hands with him, like Indian—Indians shake hands. I want to shake hands with Jesus, I want to see the beautiful flowers. Course, if it's possible that I can see Jesus, God, foremost, that's what I want. To see him, to shake hands with Jesus. I want to see the beautiful surroundings, the beautiful flowers, that's why I think I prepared myself for that.

I just love harp music! It just makes me think of angels in heaven, that harp. Because the Bible talks about harp, you don't hear about ukulele or guitar playing, they talk about harp. And I guess that's the reason. One time an Indian organization invited all those Indians that could come to see this Indian lady. She played the harp. I tell you I just sat and watched her, every time she played that harp, I watched her. So gracefully she touched the strings, and they come out music.

So I thought, I need to straighten up. I never drink, I never smoke, but anybody can do that. To really straighten your life out and believe, that's the main thing. So, when this Assembly of God pastor, Sister Grace, came along, I talked it over with her. She said, it's you, individually, how you feel. I said, "I'm getting up in years. For some reason, I want to be washed. Completely washed, not just sprinkled." She said, "Well, I can do that." I said, "Well, I'll think about it."

It took me several years, more than five years, to think about it. I studied and studied—you know, a lot of people don't believe in second baptism. I didn't know whether the Mennonites do or not, I didn't question them. It was my own self, whether I was to do right or wrong. I know it couldn't be wrong—because immersion, that's another form of baptism. And baptism is what they teach in the Bible. Jesus was baptized. I've seen pictures of him where he was standing up, where John the Baptist baptized him—it don't say he was immersed. John baptized him—how? That I could never understand, because I see pictures where he's standing up and the dove above.

For me it was hard to understand which was the right way. It was coming in my later years in life, "Well, that's enough pleasure you have had. Prepare yourself—what you believe." I've believed all my life. When I was baptized at twelve years old, I guess I believed then or I wouldn't have been baptized. And knowing that I would have something to depend on, to pray and ask for help, to provide something to eat, provide clothes for me, lead me in the right way. I believed that way, because I was brought up in a poor way.

My mother's husband, well, I couldn't say he was a farmer—he was a hunter, I guess, because Indians didn't farm. He just more or less hunted and then had a small garden—but not fields of corn or wheat like the white people have. My mother, she finished tenth grade at Haskell Indian School.

But I had drinking parents. We had a home, but it wasn't a home where we could be together every day and be happy. It was just a roof over my head. I was sad, and yet I knew, I knew that there was God, I knew that there was Jesus, but as a young person, there's a doubt. "How can he give me clothes? How can he give me food on my table?" I was thinking of the human side, see? I was thinking, I need to pray and he'll provide—I wasn't that strong a person. I wasn't a strong Christian like that until later years.

I never give up on my Christianity. I just kept going, going, going. I wanted to find out more, more. All my life, he was blessing me, he was taking care of me. I was not molested, I was not abused, even if I had drinking parents. After I got up in years, I realized the spiritual power of Jesus was taking care of me. I slept in somebody else's house, to be protected. Maybe I didn't want to, but maybe the spirit wanted me to be away from them. I didn't have that much to eat at home because they took the money for drinks. I went to live with my relatives and I went to boarding school. And there, I had clothing to wear, I wasn't alone, I had a bed. Jesus was taking care of me all through my life. And I, not really understanding, I went to church once a week, and maybe I'd be sitting there and maybe I wouldn't listen and maybe I'd be fumbling hands or something. I didn't take anything seriously, not knowing, all these blessings were given to me through Jesus.

So, after I grew up and grew older, well, I've told my people, "Go to church, read your Bible! Even if you don't understand it, read it!" I don't understand it but I read it, I have faith in it that what I'm reading about is going to come before me, is going to tell me some way. The spirit is going to show me what it means, what I'm reading about.

I just went to ninth grade, I'm not a high school graduate, I can't think things through, I ain't got that powerful mind. But I said it was Jesus and the Holy Spirit kept taking care of me. I didn't even have money when I was growing up, didn't know what it was to have money.

When I got older I thought, "You're getting up in years. Prepare yourself. Be ready to meet your Lord." That thought just come upon me, so I told my preacher, "I want to be immersed—however a person is baptized is all right, but for me I want to be immersed." My preacher, he's not a Mennonite, and yet he was sent here as an Indian preacher to be with us. I was baptized with a sprinkle on my head, so he said, "We can do that." So two years ago, July 23, 1993, we went down. "Be ready," he said. So I got ready.

I was the only one going to be immersed, and pretty soon there were two Arapahos, I think—we got two from the other church. When we walked out there, I said to the preacher's wife, "Amelia, how am I supposed to be dressed?" "Oh," she said, "Just put on shorts, not real short, and wear old tennis shoes, because there might be broken glass out there in the lake. Just wear a shirt," she said, "You don't have to dress up, you gonna be wet. But take a blanket, make somebody carry a blanket for you cause you gonna be all wet when you get out."

And when I was going to be baptized, I said to my sister-in-law, Mary Little Coyote, sing "Jesus, I'm Coming to Your Way, I Want to Follow Your Road." I had her singing that song.

So, my granddaughter Tweety, she was just all nervous, you know—this was an experience for her, too, to see this kind of baptism at the lake. And you know when I followed the preacher and his wife, there were five people to be immersed along with me. There were four women and then one man, five of us were baptized, and that was, I tell you that was a feeling. I never . . . ! I *died!* Amelia, she's a preacher herself, she was on that side of me, she said, "I'm gonna baptize you, and Newton, he'll hold you up, he won't drop you." So, I said, "All right." She said, "It won't be long, I'll just immerse you and bring you back." "All right," I said, and don't you know, when she got hold of my nose, put me under, I died. And then she brought me back, I come back alive. But I didn't explain it to her, until later on, I told her, I *died,* I just know I was dead—put in a grave, you might say. I was put in a grave. I was dead and I was put in a grave and I come alive—when the air hit me I come back alive! That was the experience that I had when I was immersed here at the lake.

And ever since then, I'm beginning to believe more, believe more. And I was feisty, I was mean. I could hurt your feelings, just say something to you. You know, I was that kind, mean. I didn't mean to be, but that was the devil in me. People were afraid of me that I might say something sarcastic to them. And I knew it. And why did I say it? And so, after that, I don't care what wrong anybody does to me, I don't care what they say about me, I always go back and I put out my hand, I just say, "How are you today?" I don't mention what was said, don't even mention it—I forget it.

Just the other day, I had a fuss with a lady on the phone. Then, I sat down over there about twenty minutes later, just smiling, you know, thinking, "That wasn't true, that come from devil's work, devil's work." So, I sat down, and I prayed and I asked the Lord to forgive. I said, "That wasn't from her, that's from the devil." And I said, "Thank you for prayer. Amen." And then I said, Get away devil! I don't want you! Get out of here, out of my house, I don't want you!" And that same evening I called that lady. So everything's all right.

The Bible, I believe it. I believe, I got my faith in it, but I could not preach it, never. Like Billy Graham, I like him. Simple, simple, and you understand what he says about the Bible. But I just recommend it to people to read it, to people that's lost, my people.

At the graveside, I sing songs like "Amazing Grace," it's got Cheyenne words in it. And we have our own tune, put Cheyenne words in it, they were inspired by, you know, to make those songs, not everybody makes them.

As much as I sing, I never was inspired, I wasn't given that talent to make a song. I guess I don't have that, but after I hear it and learn it, then I don't forget it. I sing it. But I never did make up a song. But that lady they call Belle Rouse that made lot of them church songs, she studied music when she went to school at Haskell or Chilocco, whatever, I think it was Chilocco, but she studied music, and she knew the notes and she put Indian words into them notes. She made lot of those songs.

And Frances Goose, she learned from Belle, they used to be together, she learned from Belle. They told me that they learned to sing that way in the Pentecostal Church. And they said one day, "Let's go to church." They'd bead together, and that evening they went and looked for a church to go to. And she said, "We come to this church where black people were just singing, and we went in there and we listened to them and we used to go back and listen to them." I guess that kind of roused them up to make songs, too, that's where Frances and Belle learned.[1]

I never did go to a Pentecostal church. I went to the Assembly of God over there to town. This Indian church over here, she used to want me to come, but it was more for younger ladies. And she got them to going to church, and interested in church, because the Mennonite Church in Seiling is mostly old people, old folks.

I love this Mennonite Church, and I've worked in it. One time they had this big meeting, a big conference with people from all over the world there, and I went. And they had me up on this platform, so I could see. And they took all those people, all different

1. Compact disc selections 20 and 21: "Hahoo, Ma'heo'o, Nemeo'o Nane-he'anone" (Thank You, God, we follow your way) and "Tse'oetsetanovo" (When I was troubled), melodies and texts attributed to Frances Goose; transcriptions 13 and 14 (hymns 108 and 97), appendix C.

colors, and they asked them to stand up, and walk around. And I watched them, all colors of people, and it was so beautiful. And I turned to the man who was leading the conference, and I said something, and he said, "I want you to say that to all the people." So he put me up to the microphone and I said, "How beautiful is God's creation. Why can't we get along?"

Chapter Six

Leaving Everything Behind

Time has taken its toll on Bertha's health and relationships. Her Indian name, Sunset, is significant to this stage of her life, and she reflects upon what and whom she will be leaving behind when she dies.

While reviewing the circumstances of her birth, she puzzles over traits stemming from her half-white blood and white government school environment. Health uncertainties are an increasing concern, so she has formulated a methodology for reviewing her past: she is writing her obituary.

As she thinks about her relatives, she dwells upon the meaning of relatedness, describing the rationale and method for adopting relatives outside of the family. Filling empty family places with adopted relatives has long been a Cheyenne custom; Bertha is bereft over the recent death of her son Clifford, his empty place as yet unfilled. Telling us she gave away his things, she describes other traditional mourning practices, such as cutting hair, planning a memorial dance, and maintaining the family graves. She reviews her stock in treasured adoptive relationships, including author Peter Powell and her brother Bernard Albaugh, and sings a giveaway song with words declaring that material things can be given away with ease, but death takes away that which is truly valuable.

As Bertha contemplates death, she struggles over the dedication of this book, her giveaway of songs and memories. Sustained by faith, she anticipates seeing Jesus and vividly describes a joyful journey to heaven.

My Indian name is En-o-ze. It means "sunset." There was a Cheyenne man name of Leonard Stoneroad who showed me the sign for my name: palm up over head. "You're leaving everything behind," he said. Sunset is the time of day when you're leaving everything behind. That's my name.

I think I am an illegitimate child, half white. I got white man ways, and not because I went to school under supervision, but I carry that underarm odor that white people do. There's my light complexion, my brown hair, and my way, my life, is more towards white ways. I went to school, you know, eight years of my school-year life under white supervision, and I picked up a lot of white man ways that way. Christianity, I picked that up there. But I respect all of these Indian ways. I love my Indian people.

I was born near Cantonment in Dewey County—Cantonment, Oklahoma, on February 3, 1912. I'll be eighty-five my next birthday, and the way they're treating my heart, it's like they're afraid of it. They're taking care of it—they even put a nitroglycerin patch on my arm—I don't like it, it itches. I take nine pills, different kinds. I got this oxygen I put on. It's got a long cord, but I don't like to drag it. Indian Health, they gave me hearing aid, they gave me glasses, they gave me teeth, all artificial. I don't wear them.

After I pray at night, I connect to that oxygen machine, harness my ears, ready to go to sleep and maybe if I wake up at two or three o'clock I adjust it. So all this, I have in mind that I'm going up there to the newspaper one of these days, that's what I have in mind to do, to write my obituary.

I'm going to write my obituary. I don't want Black Beard, my foster father's name, on there, because he was not my father, and I don't know how to word it to include him. And everybody knows that. Also my first husband, I sure don't want that man in there.

That's why I want to write my own obituary, because other people, they don't know my business.

I will put all my good friends down, people that have recognized me as a friend—I want to put them all in my obituary. I might want to take this Virginia to be my own daughter, but I can't because she belongs to everybody. I would want her all to myself. In my home, she could come in here and ask me for things just like my own daughter.

To adopt a relative—what it means? Possibly it's the love that you have for a deceased person. You see somebody that you think would very well represent that person, not in looks but in actions, maybe. Maybe the greetings they give you, and the way that they treated you, all this. Or you have a feeling that your deceased relative used to teach you that way, was nice to you like that, and it meant a lot to you. And possibly that's the reason that people acknowledge somebody, take somebody as a relative.

Well, there's no two people alike, no one who you can take to fulfill emptiness in your heart—to replace that empty place. Maybe she looks like your daughter, and then you long for that person to notice you as your own child would. When your child comes in, "Hello, Mom?" This other person, they always welcome you, do things for you, do favors for you, make you glad. I guess that's why folks do adopt relatives, and sometimes they do adopt somebody that looks like their son or their daughter maybe in the face, in the stature, in the actions—sometimes they take somebody like that. There are all different ways that they can adopt somebody, because you can't, well—that love you had for that deceased person is still in your heart. You want to do what you can't—you can't bring that other one back. And you are lonely for that person, and after you adopt somebody like that, it fulfills that loneliness, like. And that's why you give away.

I lost my son Clifford this year, and I comfort myself saying, "Clifford, I'll see you pretty soon. I'm up in years, I'll be with you soon." I cry and I talk to Clifford. I took all his things out of his room, gave them away.

And when a loved one dies, two, three days after, they just now cut hair. You know, Cheyenne people are careful with hair—hair that comes out, they wad up, gather up into a ball, bury it. They never throw hair away. So, when they are grieving they unbraid their hair, and have a woman to cut hair—someone qualified as medicine woman. And they didn't cut with scissors, they used to cut it with a knife. And before that, before 1900s they used to slash their arms, make arms and legs bleed. Today they don't cut flesh but they cut hair. Somebody that has been through medicine ceremonials, you give them offering—tobacco—they'll comb your hair, they'll ask how far you want it cut. They say, "Hold it tight." And the person takes hold of it and the cutter holds the other end and cuts, and then the person buries it later.

And after a while, they have a memorial dance for that loved one. April 20, 1997—Sunday—that will be my son Clifford's memorial. There's an old song, a giveaway song that says, "My fellow men, there is nothing that can cause hardship or is difficult as death. Death is the hardest part of life." And in Indian, in Cheyenne, trying to interpret what I'm trying to say in my native language, which is Cheyenne, sometimes I cannot find an English word to fully describe the Indian words that are put in this song. But it means, anything is replaceable, but death is hard to take. You don't see that person here on earth anymore.[1]

And that's a giveaway song—they sing it if they have things to give. I never hear that song anymore—that's an old, old song. A lot of times they would give away horses, blankets, material things, and they sang this song. They never expected anything returned. You know, Indians like to give away. Indians want your friendship,

---

1. Compact disc selection 22: "Giveaway Song"; transcription 6, appendix A.

and the closer you get to being friends with them, they don't forget you.

And when you take someone for a relative, you can acknowledge that person at a dance, that you adopted them. Not always, you can just adopt them to you in your home and let him or her know. Like I wasn't adopted in a crowd, but they just acknowledged me by listening to me, and greeting me, and talking to me more so than any other. That's the way it is. Some, they bring this acknowledgement out in front of a crowd and there are some that don't. And people know. Just the way you treat that person, and you can tell your relatives, "That's my daughter, I took her." And then they treat that person like your relative.

You don't have to show off that you took this person. I know my Indian people like to show off, I mean do things in ceremony in front of witnesses. Any tribe of Indians, they like that—to do things in front of people, acknowledge in front of other people, but you don't have to, because it gets around. People tell each other.

A woman adopted my brother Bernard Albaugh to take the place of her only son, and adopted me so that her son could have a sister. She acknowledged me as her daughter, and said, "Your brother, he might come to you and ask for food, money, and you will feel like you want to help him." I gave away for him when he was Head Man Dancer. When they say "sister," that means a lot to me. I knew he was going to be dancing, so I prepared for him, to give away for him. I said, "Let me say a few words." That emcee gave me that mike and I told the people, "This Bernard Albaugh, I want to tell you how he came to be my brother." And I told them the story, and then I told them that's why I give away for him Indian way, and everybody knows, and now they say, "I saw your brother today!"

And I have another man, a white man, that took me for a mother. Father Peter Powell—he was a small man. Father Powell loves our ways. He was at Sun Dance in 1965, and I said, "Let's go search around and see if I got red and blue material and let's make him a blanket." And I did a giveaway for him on last day of Sun Dance—I gave away for him to receive an Indian name—Stone Forehead. I cooked for him, made a hole in the ground and covered it with a grill. He ate at my camp and he'd listen to the men tell stories and visit with them. Then he wrote those books, *Sweet Medicine*.[2] And he writes to me and sends me presents. "My Beloved Mother Bertha," that's what he calls me. And Mother's Day, he sends me a Mother's Day card—he took me as a mother. And he calls me that.

I consider Virginia my sister—people know that she loves me and takes me as a relative. I told her and her husband, "Come here, you have a nest. Like birds come to their nests in the spring." I got a robin, comes every year. And he walks around out there, and he lets me know he's here. And I'm so glad to see him—he tells me it's spring.

I'm ready to go whenever Jesus appears. And I've got my funeral bill all paid for—my insurance—and they used to give Cheyenne and Arapaho Indians eighteen hundred dollars for funerals. So that part is all fixed out. Nobody has to bother about paying for my funeral. But, oh, I love flowers, and I know even town people are sending flowers.

That old Cantonment School where I started school so long ago, that building was ruined—there used to be nothing left but foundation bricks. But now even the bricks have been taken away. People took them out to the cemetery to put borders on the graves there.

It's called Cantonment Cemetery. It's an all-Indian cemetery. There's some old scouts buried there, there's veterans buried there, and there's some old chiefs buried there—some important people in our tribe are buried there. There are other cemeteries, not the

---

2. Peter J. Powell, *Sweet Medicine,* 2 vols. (Norman: University of Oklahoma Press, 1979).

whole tribe is at Cantonment Cemetery, but there is where people are who lived here in Dewey and Blaine Counties.

I have relatives there: my husband, my mother, my foster father, they're buried there, and my grandchildren, they're buried there. That was the only place that we could bury our people. It used to belong to the Mennonite ministry from the Mennonite Conference from Newton, Kansas. We as members, we used to take care of that cemetery.

Every Memorial Day, we'd take care of it, clean it up so it'd look clean. Lot of those tombstones at Cantonment are old chiefs, and prominent people of the tribe. Their pictures were on those tombstones, the relatives had pictures fixed on the tombstones of their loved ones. Those pictures are just maybe, no more than three inches, and some are oval, and there's some that's square. They're not very big pictures, of course—you can't put a very big picture in a tombstone. And somebody came in here in January and took all those pictures off. And nobody knows who done it. But it's a shame that somebody would steal a picture off of these tombstones. Mostly it was the pictures of Indian people that had Indian regalia on, or were elderly, with long hair, braids. Some were dressed in their buckskin clothes. Anyway they had their pictures on them tombstones and somebody took them off.

It could be antique dealers, somebody that thought they could sell them. It could be locally, they could be state, they could be out-of-state, we didn't know who did it. We had no proof. Nobody lives close enough to say they saw somebody there.

Some of the markers are wood, with old-fashioned crosses. Some that have kind of a point, a V-shape top, those are the Indian scouts. Then there's veterans, like my husband Horace was a veteran, he's got an army tombstone. When it's Memorial Day the American Legion from Canton always takes flags out there and puts them on the graves. And then some families put their own little flags on their veterans' graves.

In the late 1930s, '40s, we used to make paper flowers, crepe paper. Even the white people made them for the white cemeteries. And that's where we copied, and somebody learned, and we passed it on to each other, and that's the way we decorated our graves, with them. Crepe paper flowers. Now, we don't do that any more because crepe paper, you don't buy it like that, in different colors, like we used to. It's kind of scarce. Plastic flowers, silk flowers, they're plentiful.

Back when I was at Cantonment School, on Decoration Day—Memorial Day—we'd decorate the graves with wild flowers. And now on Memorial Day I bring flowers and clean off my graves.

See this, all this around Cantonment, is all white man land now. There's no Indian settlement here. No trees here. All wheat, all level. See how they cheated us. They didn't just cheat, they stole! They stole it! They stole a lot of Cheyenne and Arapaho lands and they call us "poor things, poor things." Sure, they made us poor. Let us have some more land, then we wouldn't be so poor.

I'm up in years, I'm eighty-four and I'm ready to go. That's why I say I go whenever that church meets—I prepare myself. I've got so hard of hearing now—some people just mumble, you know. I'm kind of showing my age and getting around just lazy. But I watch television. I sure do like to watch golf. I don't understand it, but it sure relaxes me. I just say, "Come on, ball! Come on, ball!"

The tribes have a big bingo hall, the Lucky Star. They invited all the tribal members to the opening. That's the only time I was there. Even if they say, "Go play bingo, we're gonna let you win a thousand dollars," I'd say, "No way." No way! I'd rather earn an honest ten dollars. But they sure got a lot of pretty paintings up there that local Indians painted.

I go to dances at Watonga, Fonda, all over. Every weekend there's three or four dances. All over. And at our Indian dances we don't hold hands and rub stomachs like white people. We dance by the beat of the drum, you know—we know the songs. God didn't tell us to always be sad and not mingle with people.

I had so many people involved in my life that I wouldn't know—who would be appropriate to dedicate this book to? I have so many good friends, so many relations. I have my family that I love. And I have this Mennonite Church that I belong to.

I've never been asked about dedicating anything to anybody. I don't know what it all means. If I dedicate this book, some Cheyenne's going read it and they're going to say, "She didn't make those songs. Why did she dedicate this to one or to her family?" They're very critical, my people. And they'd know that I didn't make these songs, of course I'd tell them that I was inspired to learn them, through the spirit to learn them, and then I'm called on to come lead the church songs.

These Indian church songs, they're not hard to learn, there's lots of white people want to learn them. My voice is a poor thing, so ragged. And I can't sing with those ladies at the drum anymore—I give out!

But singing songs, I want to share them, share with anybody, because they're supposed to go out, let people sing them, share, that's part of our Christianity. Now people that make songs, I'm sure they dedicate their songs to some individual, but I can't do that, because I didn't make them, I'm just singing them.

So, I would say, I would say, I leave all these songs in this book in memory of myself to be sung to anybody, and to Cheyennes that want to sing them. Because I used to enjoy and love to sing them. I didn't compose any of them.

Cheyennes have no Indian word for Jesus. He is Jesus to us, we call him Jesus. I love a song called "God Has Sent His Son to Us." To me that song is Easter—it makes me think of Easter. "God has sent his son to us"—that's some of the words in it. And at the end it says,

> If you have a burden to bear,
> If you have a burden to bear,
> Jesus calls us to come to him,

Bring it to him.
He's calling us,
Jesus is calling us.
If you have a burden, Jesus is calling,
Is calling us, come to Him.[3]

So, I keep on, I always trust the Lord to help me think things through. If I can't make it do, I try something else. Instead of crying, I push. And I want people not to forget that there's no curse words in Cheyenne.

So I guess you could say about this book, I leave this in memory of myself to my family that I love, and the Mennonite Church and its pastors and workers that kept me in line with my belief as a Christian.

My favorite color is purple. I guess I just like purple, purple flowers, material, clothing, I like it—that's my first choice. That's why that undertaker, Mr. Redinger, said, "Bertha likes purple so much, that's why I'm gonna see if I can't get her a purple casket!"

I believe when we die, we are taken up. Where I land, I don't know, but I'm hoping I land in heaven. I'm not afraid. I've heard noises in my house sometimes—fooling with my dishes, a whistle. Spirits. But I'm not afraid—I am a spirit. I saw myself as a spirit—it was in a dream—I was floating up.

When I'm buried, I want to wear a purple nightgown and purple robe. You see, a nightgown represents going to sleep, and I'm going to wake up in heaven. No silk dress, I'm not going to party. No buckskin dress, I'm not going to dance. I'm going to sleep. Don't put moccasins on my feet—I'm not going to walk, I'm not going to fly. I'm going to float!

---

3. Compact disc selection 23: "Ehane He'ama Hee'haho E'anòhemeanosesto" (Our Father above sent his son down), melody and text attributed to Belle Rouse; transcription 15 (hymn 26), appendix C.

Appendix A

Song Transcriptions

The song transcriptions and translations in this appendix originally appeared in *Southern Cheyenne Women's Songs*.[1] Please refer to the orthography chart provided in Fig. 1 as a guide to pronunciation of the song texts.

Song text translations consist of four parts: (1) translation of song text into ordinary spoken Cheyenne, (2) song text reflecting any changes between spoken language and sung language, (3) word-for-word translation, and (4) free translation to make the meaning clearer to English speakers.

A comparison between the song texts as they are spoken and as they are sung reveals a recurring pattern. Many Southern Cheyenne words contain unvoiced or whispered vowel sounds; when sung, these whispered vowel sounds are voiced, becoming new syllables.

The word endings that are ordinarily unvoiced when spoken but that are transformed by voicing when sung are highlighted on the text charts by italicized boldface type. Vocables ("chant" syllables) that are not part of definable words are in regular italics.

1. Virginia Giglio, Southern Cheyenne Women's Songs (Norman: University of Oklahoma Press, 1994).

Because the Cheyennes have no indigenous music notation system, I have transcribed the songs into standard Western European notation. Some nuances of Indian songs have no traditional Western European symbols; therefore, it was necessary to make adjustments in standard notation in order both to accommodate Cheyenne musical qualities and to remove implication of rigid concepts of key or time signature (see Fig. 2).

Fig. 1. Orthography Used in Giglio's Transcriptions

Vowels

a	as in t*a*lk or c*a*ll
ạ	*a* blended with preceding consonant and whispered
i	as in p*i*t
ī	as in the pronoun *I*
ị	*i* blended with preceding consonant and whispered
o	as in h*o*ly
ô	as in *ou*ght; also written as *au*
ọ	*o* blended with preceding consonant and whispered
u	as in m*u*ltiply
ə	English schwa sound as in b*a*nan*a* (bənanə)
ə̣	schwa blended with preceding consonant and whispered
~	appearing over two vowels indicates upward change in pitch

Consonants

b	used interchangeably with *p*
d	as in *d*ome; used interchangeably with *t*
g	as in gi*g* (sounded softly)
h	as in *h*ot
k	as in *k*eep
kha	as in a blend of *k* as in *c*all and *ha* (soft palate)
khi	as in a blend of *k* as in *c*all and *hi* (high soft palate)
kho	as in blend of *k* as in *c*all and *ho* (soft palate)
m	as in *m*ine
mha	*ma* blended with *ha* (through nose)
mhi	*ma* blended with *hi*
n	as in *n*o
p	soft *p* as in *p*ivot
s	sharp sound as in *s*o
ss	soft sound as in ni*c*e

ssh	soft sound as in *sh*e
sh	sharper sound, almost as in *ch*ip with stress on *s*
sk	as in a*sk*
t	as in *t*alk; used interchangeably with *d*
v	as in *v*ivid (also can be pronounced as *w*)
vh	blend of *v* and *h* to sound like *wh*oa but with distinct *v* sound
y	as in *y*odel or bo*y*
z	as in pi*ts,* or doubled as a separate syllable

NOTE: This chart is based on the pronunciation key from "Modern Southern Cheyenne," by Lenora Hart, developed for the Department of Education, Southern Cheyenne and Arapaho Tribes, Concho, Oklahoma. Correspondence with English vowels is approximate.

Fig. 2. Notation Symbols Used in Giglio's Transcriptions

F sharp throughout; no key or scale implication

pitch lowered by no more than a quarter tone

portamento into note from above

portamento into note from below

portamento fades downward to indeterminate pitch

portamento between notes

indeterminately pitched slide downward

indeterminately pitched slide upward

accent

Transcription 1
Hand Game Song, "Flying Around"

(Transcribed one-half step up from recording; ♩ = 90 is about
half-speed from usual performance tempo.)

1. As spoken
   Zi do ii via̱, zi do ii via̱,
   Na no o si yo ii via̱. *(repeat)*

2. As sung
   Zi do ii via̱, zi do ii via̱
   Na no o si yo*o* ii via̱,
   Na no o si yo*o* ii via̱. *(repeat)*

3. Translation
   zi do —this one
   ii via̱ —flying, flying around
   na —this, this thing, what (I'm hiding)
   no o si yo —hand game

4. Free Translation
   This one's flying around,
   This one's flying around,
   This hand game thing, this hiding thing,
   is flying around!
   This hand game thing, this hiding thing,
   is flying around!

Transcription 2
Hand Game Song, "Crows and Magpies"

1. As spoken
   O go gi mo i ha ni
   zo i ha o
   ma no o si yo ni vi vo zi

2. As sung
   O go *gi o o*
   mo *o* i ha *ni hi*
   zo i ha *o no*
   ma no o si yo ni vi vo *zi hi*

3. Translation
   o go gi —crows
   mo i ha ni —magpies
   zo i ha o —they will fly
   no o si yo —hand game
   ni vi vo zi —modifies "hand game" to "hand-gaming"

4. Free translation
   Crows and magpies will fly in when I'm hand-gaming!
   They will fly in when I'm hand-gaming!

Transcription 3
Sweetheart Song

1. As spoken

 Nī mi o o̲, hi no vi dī no o̲
 na doo sīī hi hum mi̲
 voo zi̲ vī ni vi hī ma zi̲.

2. As sung

 Chant:
 I ya i ya
 Hi yi a hi i ya hi yi,
 A hi ya ya o hi yi
 A hi yi o
 O hi yo hi yi,
 Yo hi yo hi yi
 A hi ya ho o i yo hi.

 Text:
 Nī mi *i o o*, hi no vi dī no *o,*
 Na doo si hum mi *a hi yi o*[2]
 Hi ya hi yi,
 Voo *zi* vī
 Ni vi hī ma *zi ya hi ya.*

 Chant:
 I ha i ya
 hi yi a hi
 ya o i ya hi yi,
 Hi ya i ya
 hi yi a hi
 i ya hi yi,

2. This line of text (Na doo si hum mi") is formed from an elision of the words "Na doo sīī" and "hi hum mi̲."

ya hi i ya i yi
A hi yi o hi ya hi yi,
Yo i ya hi yi a hi
yo o i ya hi
i o hi yoy.

Text:
Nī mi *i o o,* hi no vi dī no *o,*
Na doo si hum mi *a hi yi o*
Hi ya hi yi,
Voo *zi* vī
Ni vi hī ma *zi ya hi yi.*

3. Translation
   nī mi o o̱ —sweetheart; boy- or girlfriend
   hi no vi dī no o̱ —be brave; have courage
   na —I
   na doo sīı̃ —I am going
   hi hum mi̱ —get married
   voo zi̱ vi —even though
   ni vi —four
   hī ma zi̱ —spouses; husbands

4. Free translation
   Sweetheart, take courage,
   I'm going to marry you even though you're my fourth man.

   Bertha Little Coyote:
   "I don't care, go ahead and have four husbands if
   you want."

Transcription 4
Lullaby

A ho ma ho ho - a ho ma ho,

ho - ho - - - , A ho ma ho

ho - , A ho ma ho ho - ho, A ho

ma ho ho - ho - ho - A ho a ho

ho - ho - , A ho ma ho ho - ho

1. As spoken
   Vocables: *a, ma, ho*

2. As sung
   Vocables: *a, ma, ho*

3. Translation
   Syllables used in Cheyenne lullabies

4. Free translation
   Bertha Little Coyote calls this "just chant."

Transcription 5
War Song, "God Is With Me"

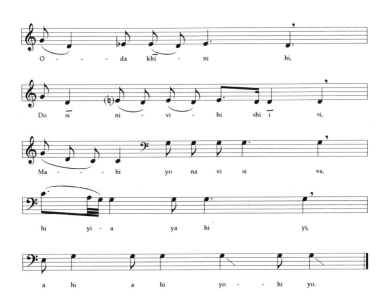

1. As spoken
    Ma i̱ vi ho i̱,
    Do sī ni vi hi shi ī si̱,
    Ma hi yo na vi si vi vi̱.
    O da khī ni̱,
    Do sī ni vi hi shi ī si̱,
    Ma hi yo na vi si vi vi̱.

2. As sung
    Chant:
    Ya hi yi a ya hi yi,
    A hi yi a ya hi yi,
    A hi yi a ya hi yi,
    Hi yi a ya hi yi,
    A hi a yi yo hi yo.

    Text:
    Ma ***i*** vi ho ***i***, *hi,*
    Do sī ni vi hi shi ī ***si***,
    Ma hi yo na vi si vi ***va***,
    Hi yi a ya hi yi,
    A hi a hi yo hi yo.

    Chant:
    (repeat previous chant section)

    Text:
    O da khī ***ni***, *hi*
    Do sī ni vi hi shi ī ***si***
    Ma hi yo na vi si (*) ***va***,
    Hi yi a ya hi yi,
    A hi a hi yo hi yo.
    *"vi" left out by singer on second verse.

3. Translation

  ma i̱ —red

  vi ho —white man

  ma i̱ vi ho —red white man; German

  do sī —where

  ni —you

  vi hi shi ī si̱ —run for life, seek refuge

  Ma hi yo —God

  na —me

  vi si vi vi̱ —is there with

  o da khī ni̱ —slit (eyes); Japanese

4. Free translation

  German, where can you seek refuge?

  God is with me.

  Japanese, where can you seek refuge?

  God is with me.

Transcription 6
Giveaway Song

1. As spoken
   O va hi
   si sto vi ho vī hi
   i sī ho do va ni ta ni̦
   o va nii hii sto ve̦ na ni
   i ho do va na do̦

2. As sung
   Chant:
   I ya hi ya,
   Hi ya hi yi
   O vi yo hi yi,
   I ya hi ya
   I ya hi yo,
   I ya hi yi a ya
   Hi yo hi yi
   Ho vi yo hi yi,
   I ya hi yo
   I ya hi hi ya,
   A hi yo hi ya hi yi
   O vi o hi yoy.

   Text:
   O va hi *ha,*
   Si sto vi, *yo hi yi,*
   Ho vī hi *hi yi hi yi,*
   I sī ho do va nī ta **no** *hi yi,*
   Ho vi yo hi yi,
   O va nii sto, va nii sto na ni,[3]

---

3. The line "nii sto, va nii sto na ni" is a combination of "nii hii sto ve̦" (death; dying) and "na ni" (our). See also the corresponding line in the second text section.

I ho do va na **do**
Vi yo hi yi yoy.

Chant:
I ya hi ya,
A ya hi yi
Ho vi yo hi yi,
I ya hi ya
Hi ya hi yo,
I ya hi ya hi ya
Hi yo hi yi
Ho vi yo hi yi yi,
I ya hi ya,
Hi ya hi hi yi,
I ya hi ya,
Hi ya i ya
Ho vi yo hi yi yoy.

Text:
O va hi *ha,*
Si sto vi, *yo hi yi,*
Ho vī hi *hi yi hi yi,*
I sī ho do va nī tan, *o hi yi,*
Ho vi yo hi yi,
O va nii sto, va nii sto na ni,
I ho do va na do
Vi yo hi yi yo.

3. Translation
   o va hi —all on earth; my fellow men
   si sto vi —things
   ho vī hi —nothing
   i sī —it is

ho do va ni ta ni̱ —not difficult
o va —except
nii hii sto ve̱ —death; dying
na ni —our
i ho do —it is
va na do̱ —difficult

4. Free translation
Bertha Little Coyote: "My fellow men, there is nothing that
can cause hardship or is difficult as death. It's the hardest
part of life."

Appendix B

Melodic Transcriptions of Forty-Nine, Round Dance, Scalp Dance, and War Dance Songs

The song transcriptions and formal analyses in this appendix originally appeared in "Transcription and Formal Analysis of Southern Cheyenne Songs," by Daniel Houston Hodges.[1] Please refer to Fig. 3 for special notation symbols used by Hodges in his transcriptions.

Note that during Hodges's research for his dissertation he consulted with Mr. Roy Nightwalker, now deceased, concerning performance practice and analysis of these particular songs from the Indian Records recording *Seventeen Southern Cheyenne Songs*.

---

1. Ph.D. diss., University of Oklahoma, 980. Available from University Microfilms International, 300 North Zeeb Road, Ann Arbor, Michigan 48106, telephone (800) 521-0600.

Fig. 3. Notation Symbols Used in Hodges's Transcriptions

+   over note. Tone slightly higher than indicated pitch. (c. 1/4 tone)

—   over note. Tone slightly lower than indicated pitch. (c. 1/4 tone)

⌢   over note. Tone slightly longer than indicated note.

⌣   over note. Tone slightly shorter than indicated note.

×   Pitch of the tone uncertain. Used also for drum accompaniment on the introduction.

Pulsations on a tone; these usually sound like rapid successions of repeated eighth or sixteenth notes, but without breaking the tones completely.

\ /   Glide/Glissando.

A, B, etc.   Major melodic divisions. Variants are shown with numerals (A1, B2, etc.)

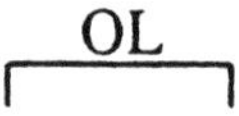

OL   Overlapping phrases. Beginning of a phrase overlaps end of preceding phrase.

Transcription 7
Forty-Nine Song

A A B B repeat as 2nd stanza, overlap to 3rd.
A A B B repeat as 3rd stanza, overlap to 4th.

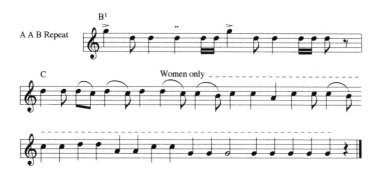

B repeats to conclude the 4th stanza.   Last cadence is shortened by one beat.

A gradual flatting causes the final stanza   to be a half-step under the indicated pitches.

Form

A A B B

A A B B

A A B B

A A B B C B

Transcription 8
Round Dance Song, "You Must Come Tonight"

B C repeat to
conclude 2nd stanza.

A3 B C repeat to
conclude the 3rd stanza.
Final cadence shortened
by 1 1/2 beats.

Form
A A1 B C
A2 A3 B C
A4 A3 B C

Transcription 9
Scalp Dance Song, "If You Turn, Would You Be
Considered a Man?"

Form
A A1 B B
A2 A3 A1 B B

Transcription 10
Scalp Dance Song, "He Fled Like a Coyote"

A1 A1 B1 C repeat as the 3rd stanza.
Three quarter notes are added to the final cadence.

A1 A1 B1 C repeat as the 4th stanza.
Three quarter notes are added to the final cadence.

Form

A1 A1 B1 C

A1 A1 B1 C

A1 A1 B1 C

Transcription 11
War Dance Song

B C B1 C1 repeat to complete 2nd stanza.

OL
A1 A B C B1 C B1 C1 repeat as the 3rd stanza.
(Note extra B1 C1 at end of 3rd stanza.)

<u>Form</u>

A A B C B1 C1
A1 A B C B1 C1
A1 A B C B1 C1 B1 C1

Appendix C

Cheyenne Hymns

The song transcriptions and translations in this appendix originally appeared in *Tsese-Ma'heone-Nemeotȯtse: Cheyenne Spiritual
Songs*. The acknowledgments in this hymnal contain the following statement: "Bertha Little Coyote of Seiling, Oklahoma, has
a gift of remembering Christian hymns from her childhood. She
has recalled hymns sung many years ago by Two Crows, Red-
bird Black, and Watan. She contributed these hymns to this
hymnbook." Bertha is also listed as a member of the editorial
committee.[1]

Please note that song texts appear in a different orthographic
system than those in appendix A (see orthography chart, Fig. 4).
The Cheyenne orthography used in these hymns has evolved from
a system developed by Rodolphe Petter in 1891; stages of devel-
opment to its present form have included work by scholars at the
Summer Institute of Linguistics at the University of Oklahoma
and linguists associated with the Northern Cheyenne Bilingual

---

1. David Graber, ed., *Tsese-Ma'heone-Nemeotȯtse: Cheyenne Spiritual Songs*
(Newton, Kans.: Faith and Life Press, 1982), 193. This hymnbook and accom-
panying tapes are available from the Cheyenne Christian Education Project
(CCEP), Box 50, Busby, Montana 59016, telephone (406) 592-3643.

Education Program. Missionary-linguists Wayne and Elena Leman collaborated with hymnologist David Graber and a team of Cheyenne consultants to compile this hymnal.

A few special notation symbols, shown in Fig. 5, are used in the hymns. The hymn numbers given are those by which they are listed in *Tsese-Ma'heone-Nemeotòtse.*

Fig. 4. Orthography Used in Cheyenne Hymn Texts

a	as in	"f*a*ther"
e	as in	"p*i*t" or in "p*e*t"
h	as in	"*h*ot"
k	as in	"s*k*in"
'	as in	"oh-oh"; glottal stop
m	as in	"*m*other"
n	as in	"*n*ot"
o	as in	"b*o*ne"
p	as in	"s*p*in"
s	as in	"*s*ick"
š	as in	"*sh*ip"; this letter is called "esh"
t	as in	"s*t*ick"
v	as in	"*v*et" or in "*w*et"
x	as in	German "A*ch*tung!"
'		high stress mark (sound pitched higher)
.		over vowel, a whisper mark
-		meaning-separation mark; divides words into morphemes

SOURCE: This chart is based on the pronunciation key from the *English-Cheyenne Student Dictionary* produced by the Language Research Department of the Northern Cheyenne Title VII ESEA Bilingual Education Program in Lame Deer, Montana.

Fig. 5. Special Notation Marks Used in Hymns

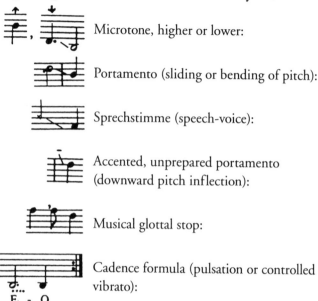

Microtone, higher or lower:

Portamento (sliding or bending of pitch):

Sprechstimme (speech-voice):

Accented, unprepared portamento (downward pitch inflection):

Musical glottal stop:

Cadence formula (pulsation or controlled vibrato):

SOURCE: Graber, *Tsese-Ma'heone-Nemeotòtse*, 198–99.

Transcription 12
"Jesus, Venave'hoomemeno" (Jesus, look now on us)
Hymn 122

Cheyenne hymn attr. to Paul Littleman, 1913-1974
Based on a Kiowa hymn attr. to Lena Sheridan, c. 1950

Kiowa melody

♪ = 176

Je - sus A,*   ve - na - ve' - ho - o - me - me - no!   Ve - nanè - še - va - ta - me - me - no!
Jesus,   *look now on us!*   *Be merciful now to us!*

Ne - me - o - 'o   tse - me - tse - me - no - to   na - noo - se - no - vàhe - no - ne,
Your way   *that you gave to us*   *we do not live up to it,*

Neh - vah - to - menè - še - va - ta - me - me - no!
Yet be merciful to us!

Naa   ne - to - no - o - ma - tse - me - no,   Je - sus   A - HE.
And   *we wait for you,*   *Jesus.*

*Or, "Ma'heo'o, . . ."

Transcription 13
"Hahoo, Ma'heo'o, Nemeo'o Nanehe'anone"
(Thank you, God, we follow your way)
Hymn 108

Transcription 14
"Tse'oetsetanovo" (When I was troubled)
Hymn 97

Nestonevaoo'e *Frances Goose*, 1899-1952

Plains Indian melody
Attr. to Frances Goose

♩ = 76

Tse - 'oe - tse - ta - no - vo   Ma' - he - o - 'o   na - ha - oe - na' - to - vo.
When I was troubled   to God   I prayed.

Nah - ta - oe - nah - to - tse   eh - no - 'es - ta   HE - HE.
*My prayer   he answered.**

Na - ve' - še - he - to - tae - ta - no   HE - E,
This makes me happy,

Na - ve' - še - he - to - tae - ta - no   HE - E.
This makes me happy.

*Intended to mean "he answered it"; "ehno'ésta'ta."

Transcription 15
"Ehane He'ama Hee'haho E'anȯhemeanosesto" (Our Father above sent his son down)
Hymn 26

For God so loved the world that he gave his only begotten son, . . . John 3:16

Belle Wilson Rouse, 1903-1971
Based on John 3:16

Cheyenne melody
Attr. to Belle Wilson Rouse

♩ = 108

1. E - ha - ne   he - 'a - ma   HE - E
    Our Father   above

Hee' - ha - ho   e - 'a-nȯhe - me - a - no - ses - to   ho - 'e - va
    Sent his Son down   *to earth*

Tseh - me - ho - tae - tse   HE - HE,
Because he loved us,

Tses - to - se - HE - vo'ė - sta - nevė - hae - tse.
So he can save us.

2. Ve - na - o - ne'-se - o - ma - ta - ma   Je - sus   A - HE!
    Believe in   Jesus!

Ve - na - hes - ta - no - mo - va   he - ees - tses - totsė   HE - HE!
Receive   his word!

" Ne - naasėstsė   tse - haa - nao' - xe - to   HE - E
"Come,   you who have a heavy load

Tseh - ve'- šė - HE - a - no - ve - ta - notȯ havė-se,". Je-sus ne - o -noo-mae-ne.
When saddened by sin,"   *Jesus calls to us.*

Transcription 16
"Esenehane Jesus" (Our friend Jesus)
Hymn 3

... That Jesus would die ... for the scattered children of God, to bring them together and make them one.
John 11:51-52

Attr. to Ova'hehe *Mrs. Bear Bow*, 1880-1934

Attr. to Ova'hehe, 1880-1934

♩ = 132

E - se - ne - ha - ne Je - sus, E - se - ne - ha - ne Je - sus,
Our friend *Jesus,* *Our friend* *Jesus,*

Neo-noo-mae-ne, neo-noo-mae-ne, "Neh-mo-heeh-ne! Neh-mo-heeh-ne!"
He invites us, *he invites us.* *"Come together! Come together!"*

Je - sus A neo - noo - maenè, ne - naa - se!
Jesus *calls us,* *come!*

Appendix D

Compact Disc Notes

1. Story and Song, "In the Sweet By and By" (4:09)
This recording of Bertha's childhood memory of singing during a wagon ride to town allows the listener to hear her voice and experience her storytelling style.

2. Hand Game Song, "Flying Around" (1:43)
When Bertha recorded songs while sitting in her kitchen, it was difficult for her to keep her hands off the microphone. In this recording, Bertha translates the song, describes the accompanying motions, and explains the context of the hand game.

3. Hand Game Song, "Crows and Magpies" (1:36)
Bertha translates the song and gives more information about hand game and its music.

4. Sweetheart Song (1:55)
A song of flirtatious challenge.

5. Lullaby (1:25)
A song from Bertha's young womanhood, sung while breast-feeding her son, Woodrow.

6. "Fonda War Mothers Song" (2:25)
Some of Bertha's clearest memories were related to me while we took long drives in western Oklahoma. She told me to stop the car, and "Fonda War Mothers Song" was recorded beside the highway, with trucks passing us by.

7. Comments, Forty-Nine Song (2:05)
In Bertha's home, we listened together to a recording of Bertha singing in 1969; I taped her comments while she listened to the music. Now, nearly thirty years after the background music was recorded, we hear Bertha's remarks about that music, previously issued without liner notes. (Selections 9, 11, 13, and 15 also contain Bertha's remarks about songs from the record.) Here, Bertha describes something of the context and history of Forty-Nine song, the behavior of men and women at a Forty-Nine dance, and the Forty-Nine behavior of the younger generation.

8. Forty-Nine Song (2:45)
Recorded by Bertha Little Coyote in 1969.*

9. Comments, Round Dance Song (3:00)
Bertha identifies and translates the song. Bertha patiently teaches Virginia the Cheyenne words, explaining the difference between its spoken and sung Cheyenne text.

---

*Selections 8, 10, 12, 14, and 16—with Roy Nightwalker, Denny Old Crow, Hailman Little Coyote, Mary Little Coyote, and Bertha Little Coyote—were digitally remastered from a 33⅓-rpm monaural record album, *Seventeen Southern Cheyenne Songs*, originally recorded and distributed by Oscar Humphreys, Indian Records, Inc., Fay, Oklahoma 73646, telephone (405) 887-3316. Used by permission. This recording was still available in 1997.

10. Round Dance Song, "You Must Come Tonight" (1:46)
Recorded by Bertha Little Coyote in 1969.

11. Comments, Scalp Dance Song (2:21)
Bertha identifies this song from the record as a scalp dance and explains the reason for the song's designation. She translates the Cheyenne text, with particular attention to depth of meaning in terse Cheyenne phrases.

12. Scalp Dance, "If You Turn, Would You Be Considered a Man?" (1:14)
Recorded by Bertha Little Coyote in 1969.

13. Comments, Scalp Dance Text (3:10)
Bertha sings along with recorded scalp dance, then explains the text of the song sections, repeating in Cheyenne.

14. Scalp Dance, "He Fled Like a Coyote" (1:54)
Recorded by Bertha Little Coyote in 1969.

15. Comments, War Dance Song (2:19)
Bertha explains the difference between the repertoire known as War Dance songs and war songs in terms of their texts, form, and context. Other song types are classified.

16. War Dance Song (2:01)
Recorded by Bertha Little Coyote in 1969.

17. Hymn, "How Great Thou Art" (0:57)
Bertha sings an example of a hymn from non-Indian origins sung in the Cheyenne language.

18. Hymn, "Jesus, Venave'hoomemeno" (Jesus, look now on us) (2:05)

The melody of this song, recorded in Bertha's home, is one she believes was originally a peyote tune but is now used in a Christian context.

19. War Song, "God Is with Me" (2:55)
An example of a traditional Cheyenne song with a spiritual message that is not considered a church song. Bertha tells about the context in which she first heard this song and translates the text.

20. Hymn, "Hahoo, Ma'heo'o, Nemeo'o Nanehe'anone" (Thank You, God, we follow your way) (1:29)
Sung by Bertha in the Seiling Mennonite Church, with help from Pastor Amelia Old Crow.

21. Hymn, "Tse'oetsetanovo" (When I was troubled) (1:29)
Sung at the Seiling Mennonite Church during Sunday morning service. Ambient sounds are from the congregation.

22. Giveaway Song (3:57)
Bertha translates this song, explains the song's context in the giveaway tradition of the Cheyenne people, and provides insight into the meaning of possessions and of death.

23. Hymn, "Ehane He'ama Hee'haho E'anòhemeanosesto" (Our Father sent his son down) (2:03)
This is one of Bertha's favorite hymns. To her, Bertha says, this song means "Easter."

24. Hymn, "Esenehane Jesus" (Our friend Jesus) (1:36)
Bertha, Virginia Giglio, and Pastor Amelia Old Crow sing this song together at the Seiling Mennonite Church.

Index